# SAMPLERS

## Five Centuries of a Gentle Craft

## Anne Sebba

ON NEEDLEWORK

*With cheerful mind we yield to men*
*The higher honours of the pen*
*The needle's our great care,*
*In this we chiefly wish to shine*
*How far the art's already mine*
*This sampler does declare.*

Ann Wood, aged 8, Midsummer 1817.

Thames and Hudson

*For Mark*

First published in the United States in 1979 by Thames and Hudson, Inc.,
500 Fifth Avenue, New York, New York, 10036

Designed by Sara Komar for Weidenfeld and Nicolson, London
Layouts by Heather Sherratt

Library of Congress Catalog card number 79-53101

ISBN 0-500-23300-4

Filmset and printed in Great Britain by Butler & Tanner Ltd,
Frome and London

# Contents

Introduction · 6

1   The Early Examples · 13

2   England's Golden Age · 29

3   The Schoolroom Products · 55

4   America's Blossoming Tradition · 81

5   The Nineteenth Century · 113

6   Modern Samplers · 139

Cleaning Methods · 150

Glossary of Stitch Designs · 152

Select Bibliography · 156

Acknowledgements · 157

Index · 159

# Introduction

Ever since cloth has existed man has displayed a natural urge to embellish it. The word 'sampler' comes from the Latin *exemplum*, meaning 'something chosen from a number of things, a sample ... an example to be followed, a model'. By 1530 John Palsgrave's Anglo-French dictionary *Lesclarissement de la Langue Francoyse* defined not only what the object was, but who made it: 'Exampler for a woman to work by; example.' The accepted use of the word today is as a reference sheet for embroidery patterns or an experimental practice ground for stitches. Samplers from the sixteenth to the twentieth centuries have included examples of both counted thread embroidery, where the stitches are worked by counting the threads of the background material, and free embroidery, where the stitches follow free-flowing lines irrespective of the background weave of the material.

The earliest surviving example is thought to be an ancient Peruvian sampler of early Nazca culture, which has been dated approximately at between AD 200 and 500. This specimen is worked in cotton and wool on a cotton cloth and portrays some seventy-four figure motifs recorded in embroidery. They include several birds, human and mythological beings, plants, a toad, a fish and a scorpion all worked in simple running stitch. Some of the motifs overlap each other, perhaps because the need for the earlier ones had disappeared or perhaps because new motifs were added by later generations. It is impossible to know. Experts consider the piece to be either a record of design and theme or an initial step in planning and creating an embroidery. Fragments of decorated material have also been found in the tombs of the ancient Egyptians, and these illustrate that samplers have roots in the Near East as well. These examples are believed to have been made around AD 400–500 and are

An elaborate, densely worked Spanish sampler, signed and dated, 1756.

clearly early pattern samplers. The remains of an Egyptian sampler kept in the Victoria and Albert Museum in London and probably worked in the fifteenth or sixteenth century has geometrical patterns in double running and darning stitches in silk on linen and includes two motifs, the 'S' and 'X', which were soon to become a much-loved part of the European, as well as English, sampler tradition.

It is not known exactly when samplers made their first appearance in Europe. There is good written evidence that by the early sixteenth century they had become a familiar aspect of British court life – a fashionable occupation for those who could look on embroidery as a pleasurable, but none the less essential, leisure activity. There is no doubt that the early samplers were indispensable to their makers, but it is strange that none has survived from this period.

The earliest known dated sampler, an English one which came to light only in 1960, was made as late as 1598. There are two undated examples, one German and one Italian, believed to have been made earlier in the

7

century. All three were made at a time when printed pattern books, although costly and rare, were beginning to appear throughout Europe. Their appearance coincided in Britain with a flourishing of domestic embroidery as ecclesiastical embroidery began to decline and richly decorated clothing, especially for men, became the order of the day. Is it surprising, then, that romantic, literary praise heaped on the hardworking sampler-makers of the sixteenth century – who were almost all amateur, adult and female – came from grateful males? Nor is it surprising that the great revival of interest in samplers today coincides with a slow but painstaking revision of history in an effort to discover the hitherto uncharted roles of women.

From the sixteenth to the twentieth centuries thousands of women and girls in countries quite remote from each other made samplers. In some ways these were remarkably similar, containing motifs or border patterns gleaned from the early pattern books. But each country had its own peculiar traditions and the pictorial sampler, which flourished in America and to a lesser extent in Britain, never achieved the same popularity in continental Europe.

Samplers made in Spain and the Spanish colonies from the seventeenth to nineteenth centuries were large, highly elaborate pieces with a richness and sumptuous effect not seen in other examples. Spanish embroidery was often executed in fine, counted thread work in one colour only – black. Spanish blackwork was no doubt a result of the Moorish influence throughout the country's art but the technique was also popular in England, partly because it simplified copying from two-tone engravings. In Italy, the home of intricate lacework, samplers containing many examples of delicate cutwork border patterns were the most popular. In Italian, Spanish and German samplers one of the most frequent motifs was the crucifix, as well as other symbols of the Passion including the crown of thorns, ladder, hammer and nail. German and Dutch samplers usually comprised a random assortment of motifs, religious and otherwise, with little concern about design. These pieces were rarely signed in full but would probably contain a garland enclosing the maker's initials and a date. With the exception of French samplers, which most closely resemble English ones, those made in Europe rarely contained the verses or inscriptions which give English and American ones much of their appeal – especially when a child makes a spelling mistake in her own surname. But sometimes a motto such as 'Passion Christi conforta me' (Passion of Christ comfort me) might be embroidered.

Nowhere are samplers quite as long and thin as in the early English variety. But, generally, the repertoire of stitches did not differ greatly

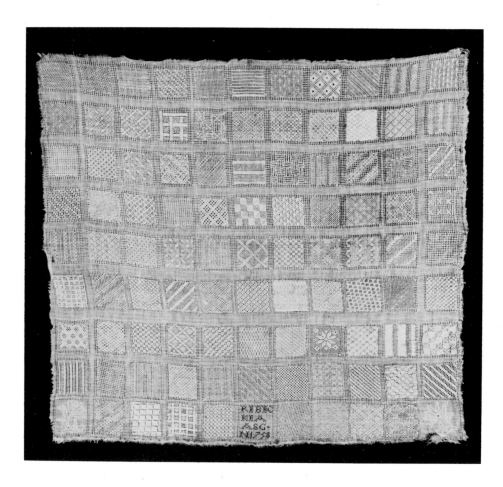

An exquisitely worked Danish sampler on muslin, 1758, in which ninety-six of the squares contain a distinct pattern in drawn and pulled work. Denmark was renowned for its tradition of superb whitework.

throughout Europe. Cross stitch was the universal favourite with some of the finest work in many other stitches being done in Spain and Italy.

Sampler-making tells us as much about the social, religious and industrial trends of the places and times at which each was made as do many history books. And it tells us this in a way at once charming and touching, often naive and a little sad. Despite the similarity of motifs down the ages, a study of English and American samplers can still lead one to intimate knowledge of the embroideress concerned. Few other objects tell us as much about their makers. We can imagine the hours and months that must have been spent in quiet dedication perfecting the techniques required for a seventeenth-century lacework sampler. We can agonize with the eighteenth-century child who, unable to make her stylized floral border turn the corner at the right place, unpicked it several times before admitting defeat, leaving holes in her cloth. And we can share the joy of countless nineteenth-century parents when confronted with their daughters' first display of expertise with a needle, recorded for posterity in a moralizing verse.

For some four centuries needlework was an essential part of a woman's

Worked by Mme Tchotanova in 1946, the borders in this Bulgarian sampler represent the districts of Samokov, Sofia and Graovo. Satin, back, buttonhole, tent, cross, running, encroaching gobelin and brick stitches on linen.

life, whether she was of the leisured upper classes who regarded fine sewing as a prized accomplishment, or of the more needy lower classes for whom plain sewing was often a means of survival in a harsh world. Many of the products of this needlework have perished, largely through overuse, but thousands of samplers have survived, testament not only to the fashion of the day but also to education and social custom. For an enormous number of samplers was made, as innumerable girls in Europe and the colonies worked at least one during their school years. Until recently they were not thought to be worth very much and when, for example, an elderly relative died, a sampler would probably have been preserved while a set of chairs or silverware would be sold. Even if they had been accounted as valuable, it might have been rather embarrassing to sell something with the family name emblazoned on it. There is no doubt that by the nineteenth century samplers had acquired some value; at least one arrived in the family of its present owner as part payment for lodgings. But, above all, the sampler was a sentimental object that had probably taken months to complete and was cherished by the maker or her family. Such a piece could not lightly be discarded. And so, although samplers may be only a by-product of the art of needlework, they have now achieved recognition in their own right, becoming highly prized collectors' items.

As with any work of art, would-be collectors should be watchful of forgeries. A sampler now bearing the name Eleanor Speed and the dates 1783 and 1784 was in fact made in 1733–34 by someone whose surname was Speed but whose first name was not Eleanor. It may be assumed that Eleanor was hoping to pass off the work of a relative as her own. Another sampler, made by L. Hart, now bears the date 1627; but since it also bears a pattern of three lines of music from a tune called 'St Peter' which was not published until 1830, this too is clearly a false date. Many a nineteenth-century needlewoman, when she reached her middle years, was coy enough to unpick the last two digits on her childhood sampler.

This book sets out to chart the growth of samplers as a minor art form in Britain and America. The fairy-tale land of samplers has always been fertile ground for imagination – from the religious symbols and classical motifs of the earliest pieces depicted in every available silk and wire thread enriched with pearls and beads, to the pictorial scenes of the eighteenth- and nineteenth-century examples where birds are bigger than the trees in which they perch, baskets of flowers grow out of a church spire, and houses, mountains and human figures all enjoy an engaging lack of perspective. The early English specimens, made at a time when standards of amateur needlework were exceptionally high, illustrate a technical dexterity with a needle and thread which is hard to better. By the eighteenth century, sampler-making in Britain had declined to become merely a school exercise, but in America samplers had thrown off their English origins and developed into an indigenous handicraft that revelled in its originality.

Today samplers are still made, both as a record of sewing methods and as an attractive way to display an important family or national event. But they are worked as a hobby or as part of a professional needlework training and do not form part of a young girl's essential education.

Samplers of any period are imbued with quaintness and charm, and convey a tender eagerness to please. They lack passion, but are alluring; they are not products of a moment's genius but rather months of effort. Above all, samplers are cast in the mould of a gentle, feminine art.

# 1

# The Early Examples

Early modern Europe was, for many, an exciting place to live. The late fifteenth and early sixteenth centuries witnessed more changes, at a faster rate, than had previously been imagined by any but the wildest dreamers. There was fresh interest in learning, and intense questioning of religious and scientific matters. Epoch-making voyages of discovery were stirring the public imagination with tales of whole new worlds from the West Indies to the Far East. Men and women travelled beyond the confines of their native regions as never before, sometimes out of curiosity, sometimes as refugees fleeing religious persecution. It was as if the world had suddenly expanded. Above all, the new liberated ideas of the Renaissance, the rebirth of belief in the potential of the individual in this world, permitted a degree of concentration on the pleasures of physical existence that would have been considered sinful and wicked by an earlier age.

Nowhere is the exuberance of sixteenth-century man and his enjoyment of life to the full more apparent than in the needlework of the day and, indeed, developments in the manufacture of cloth and its embellishments were noted with the same sense of delight accorded to change in other areas. One contemporary rhyme recorded that:

> Hops, Reformation, bays and beer
> Came into England all in a year.

Bays refers to a type of light cloth. In England there was a great tradition of fine embroidery on which to draw. Ecclesiastical embroidery, known as *opus anglicum*, had been held in very high esteem throughout Europe from the mid-thirteenth century until the end of the fourteenth. Highly sought after by monarchs and church dignatories, most of the pieces were made in the workshops of London by professional masters of the craft,

OPPOSITE Needlework was an essential skill for most women in the sixteenth century. The woman embroidering in this 1573 engraving might well have derived her geometric design from one of the printed pattern books which were beginning to be available throughout Europe.

13

both male and female. But these skills had been largely neglected for one hundred years before the new tradition of domestic embroidery came to full flower.

One of the primary reasons for the revival of interest in needlework was the enormous growth in commerce that resulted from the geographical discoveries of the age. Renaissance explorers were coming home laden with gold and spices, silver, pearls, pineapples, sweet herbs, dyestuffs, furs and many other commodities; few of those who could afford such delights were able to resist their temptations. Venice and Genoa, two ports which had once held a monopoly on world trade, were soon challenged by many other European cities quick to build up fleets of trading ships to satisfy the population's increasing appetite for luxuries. And so a new class came into being, the wealthy merchants of Europe who aspired now only to join the ranks of the aristocracy.

These merchants spent a major portion of their new-found wealth on clothes and domestic luxuries such as table and bed covers, cushions and wall hangings, many of them fashioned from the rich and varied fabrics that were imported from the East. As far as clothing was concerned, the vanity of men and women seemed to know no bounds, keen as they were to display the extent of their affluence. Men's fashions in dress changed more quickly than women's: many men displayed an infatuation with personal attire, captivated by the feel of the fabulous silks and velvets, furs, brocades and taffetas. They luxuriated in fabrics that were adorned with stitchery, gold, and precious stones. Needlework thus became both a fashionable occupation and a necessary craft for those women who had the leisure to pursue it, and many of these amateurs reached an extraordinarily high level of proficiency. There were still professional embroiderers, of course, who would execute the more elaborate work such as formal court costumes lavishly embroidered with metal threads and beads, and heraldic devices. But sometimes it is hard to tell whether a surviving piece such as a cushion or pair of gloves is the work of an amateur or professional.

Tudor amateur embroidery was originally undertaken only by the noblest ladies of the land – it was certainly necessary to have fine, smooth, white hands for such delicate, detailed work. But the Tudor monarchy, in bringing to England a return of settled conditions and a consequent increase in prosperity, had enlisted the help of the local gentry. It needed them as Members of Parliament for help in raising taxes, as Justices of the Peace for help in maintaining order and, increasingly, as civil servants. This meant that along with the rise of a wealthy merchant middle class there also grew up a gentry middle class. Both were keen to

The fourth Earl of Dorset, painting attributed to William Larkin. Men's fashions were often more lavish and more richly embellished than women's, and required painstaking attention to fine detail.

**Eyn newe kunstlich moetdelboech alle kunstner**
xo brauchen fur snytzeller/wapensticker, perlensticker, etc. vnnd ouch fur Jonferen vnd frauwe kunstlich vff das neuwes gefonde/allen den gene die vpff kunste verstar habe.
Gedruckt zo Cöllen durch Peter Quentel. Jmiair. M.D.XXIX. im Euenmaent.

The title page of Peter Quentel's *Eyn Newe Kunstlich Moetdelboeck alle Kunstner.*

consolidate their positions, which were soon as strong as the feudal baronies of the fifteenth century. These middle classes wished to copy whatever pursuits appeared fashionable among the aristocracy, and nothing was quite so much in vogue as being seen working a piece of embroidery. Needlework had already assumed first place in a girl's education, along with reading and writing, and the resultant skill was often put to much good use in furnishing Tudor households with a feeling of opulence and warmth, as well as creating small borders to adorn clothing or household linen. The amount of decorated upholstery and curtains in a house were the surest indications of a family's level of wealth.

Coinciding with the expansion of trade at this time was the development of printing methods, which was to have an equally crucial effect on needlework. Gutenberg had invented printing in Germany just before the mid-fifteenth century and in 1477 the first book published in England had been produced by William Caxton; by the mid-sixteenth century printed pattern books, mostly for cut- or lacework but also for embroidery, were spreading throughout a large area of Europe. They were costly and could be afforded only by the very rich. Almost all the

 *The Early Examples*

patterns were by male artists and were clearly intended for a female amateur audience and not the male professional embroiders of an earlier day.

Among the earliest books of which copies remain were those by Johannes Schönsperger (*c.* 1523) and Peter Quentel (1529), *Esemplario di Lavori* (1530) by Giovanni Andra Vavassore and *La Vera Perfettione del Disegno* (1561) by Giovanni Ostau – the last two were both Venetian. French publishers were next on the scene but the first book to be printed in England did not appear until 1586: *La Clef des Champs* by Jacques le Moyne. It contained patterns of birds, animals and flowers.

In 1587 Federico Vinciolo's book *Les Singuliers et Nouveaux Pourtraicts pour touttes sortes d'ouvrages di Lingerie* was published in France; it was produced in England some four years later by John Wolfe as *New and Singular Patternes and workes of Linnen*. Vinciolo, a leading Venetian designer, was a recognized master of the art of designing lace patterns for neck ruffs and sleeve cuffs and his slim little volume was reprinted at least seventeen times between 1587 and 1658, leading one to believe that the cultured and critical ladies of that era considered the book the best of its type. Dedicated to the Dowager Queen of France, Vinciolo's book was prefaced with the following sonnet:

*To the Ladies and Young Misses*

One man will strive to win the heart of some liege lord
In order to possess a sum of riches great;
Another in high rank himself would situate;
Another in the wars will seek for his reward.

But I, who only seek to keep from being bored,
Am satisfied to live in this my lowly state,
And by my labours grave strive only to create
A gift for womankind, contentment to afford.

Then, ladies, please accept (I pray you will so do)
These patterns and designs I dedicate to you,
To while away your time and occupy your mind.

In this new enterprise there's much that you can learn,
And finally this craft you'll master in your turn.
The work agreeable, the profit great you'll find.
To die unremittingly for Virtue is not to die.

But the most popular of all sixteenth-century printed pattern books as far as English workers were concerned was Johann Sibmacher's *Schön*

17

## Samplers

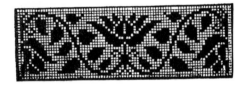

Cross stitch border patterns from Schönsperger's book of 1523 (top) and Quentel's of six years later. Duplication of designs in these pattern books was frequent.

*neues Modelbuch*, first published in Nuremberg in 1597. A number of his designs have been traced in English and American needlework as late as the nineteenth century and his patterns were reproduced in the seventeenth-century book, *The Needle's Excellency*. Other books of particular interest were those on natural history, especially botany. The embroidered wall hangings and silk and velvet cushions of the day contained many delightful representations of common and exotic species of flowers and plants, animals, insects and birds, usually executed in a very detailed manner.

An embroideress would either copy patterns herself, or, if she were rich enough, employ a professional to do this for her. Sometimes designs were copied by counting threads or square meshes but more often this was done by pricking through the outline of the motif on the printed page and then lightly dusting over the holes on to the material to be worked. The latter method, called pouncing, helps to explain why so few pattern books have survived, even though many of them enjoyed so many editions. It is also probable that well-to-do ladies would often simply tear out the leaves of a favourite pattern book and distribute them to their needlewomen.

As well as the pattern books, woodcuts, herbals and illuminated manuscripts proved a source of inspiration for the needleworker. In addition, travelling and even warfare continued to encourage a growing cultural exchange which included knowledge of fashions in textiles in other countries.

But in spite of all this, the best way to ensure that an attractive new embroidery pattern was not forgotten was to take a piece of cloth and reproduce it there. In that way one could also experiment by reproducing the motif in different coloured threads, or with a variety of stitches. These samplers, as they were called (or perhaps sam- or samp-cloths at that time), would be stitched by adult, amateur needlewomen at random with scattered patterns in no particular order. They would be rolled up and put away in a needlework case when not in use.

The sampler was essential not only for a needleworker not rich enough to buy the pattern books but also for those who wanted to avoid unnecessary wastage. The cost of materials was high and most needlewomen would need to ensure that they were familiar with working a particular design or type of thread before they started on a large project. Often they might leave the pattern unfinished as a reminder of how it should be worked. Since as many as twenty shades of one colour might be used on a major piece it was necessary to try these out together first. The most popular colours were dark and pale blue, various shades of green,

18

The simplicity and delicacy of blackwork was very popular in Tudor times. The technique was used for both household embroidery, as in the linen pillow cover above, and lavish costume, as shown in George Gower's portrait of Mary Cornwallis.

yellow, orange, brown and red. Sometimes two different coloured strands would be twisted together to give an effect of the intermediate shade.

One of the most effective types of Tudor embroidery was blackwork – a single thread of black silk on a plain white or cream linen background. Blackwork is often said to have been introduced into England by Catherine of Aragon, Henry VIII's first wife. But although she had brought

## Samplers

many examples of it with her in her trousseau, it was already being practised by the English when she arrived in 1501. When combined with gold and silver, blackwork could produce a very delicate quality that was well suited to the popular linear border patterns of ivy and vine. That it was often used to decorate the edges of white cuffs can clearly be seen from many of the contemporary paintings of Hans Holbein, among others. Because of this, a plain running stitch in a black thread used as a border is often called a Holbein stitch, although in Elizabethan blackwork a greater variety of stitch is usually to be found.

Metallic thread was also very popular. Like silk, it was expensive, but it was more difficult to use, requiring a different technique. In 1582 John Hudson of Newcastle was selling sewing silk for £1 6s. a pound, while sewing crewels (thin worsted yarn) cost only 3s. 4d. a pound. Ten years later gold for sewing cost as much as 2s. 9d. an ounce.

And so it is not surprising that the most famous of Tudor needlewomen were wealthy and titled ladies such as the young Princess Elizabeth, later to be Queen Elizabeth I, Elizabeth Hardwick, Countess of Shrewsbury, known as Bess of Hardwick, and Mary Queen of Scots. In 1544 the eleven-year-old Princess Elizabeth embroidered a book binding, now in the Bodleian Library, Oxford, as a New Year's gift for her stepmother Catherine Parr. But she progressed to finer things and all three of these women have been credited with completing many excellent embroideries and wall hangings, some of which are still to be seen in the magnificent English houses where they lived. Mary Queen of Scots was in the custody of the Earl of Shrewsbury from 1569 to 1584 and it is believed that she and Bess of Hardwick collaborated on some of their best needlework at that time.

A 1601 inventory of Hardwick Hall, the magnificent house in Derbyshire which Bess of Hardwick had built for herself after the death of her fourth and last husband, mentions that a professional 'imbroder' had been allocated both a room and an 'inner' room. Several embroiderers had been employed during the 1590s, when the Hall was being built and decorated, both to work new pieces and to repair those which Bess had brought from Chatsworth House, one of her many former homes. The inventory lists many of the embroidered objects that graced the home, including hangings of embroidery on cloths of gold, silver, tissue, and velvet. Perhaps some of these contained animal motifs from Conrad Gesner's *Historiae Animalium* (1551–58), which it is known were copied by both Mary Queen of Scots and Bess of Hardwick in some of their needlework.

It is hard for us to imagine just how valuable textiles were in

OPPOSITE One of three complete velvet hangings at Oxburgh Hall, Norfolk, whose panels are known to have been worked by Mary Queen of Scots and Bess of Hardwick. Embroidered in coloured silks on canvas, the panels contain a variety of bird, fish and animal motifs, some of which were copied from Conrad Gesner's *Historiae Animalium*.

## Samplers

sixteenth-century England and why samplers and other embroideries should have been accorded such a high place in inventories and wills. The earliest English documentary reference to samplers which has so far been noted is an item of 1502 in the Privy Purse expenses of Elizabeth of York: 'The Xth day of July to Thomas Fishe in reward for bringing of conserve of cherys from London to Windsore ... and for an elne of lynnyn cloth for a sampler for the Queen, viijd (8*d*.].' That samplers were clearly objects of value can be seen from the will of Margaret Thomson of Freeston in Lincolnshire: 'I gyve to Alys Pynchbeck my systers doughter my sawmpler with semes.' 'Semes' here probably means rows or bands of pattern – a type of sampler which was to become popular in the next century. Samplers were prized on the Continent as well; a 1509 inventory of Joan the Mad, Queen of Spain, lists some fifty samplers worked in silk and gold thread.

One of the first English pattern books specifically to mention samplers was *A Booke of Curious and Strange Inventions called the first part of Needleworkes*, published by William Barley in 1596. It included the following advice in its introduction:

> Keep cleane your samplers, sleepe not as you sit,
> For sluggishness doth spoile the rarest wit.

But literary references to samplers occur much earlier than this – a sure indication that they were popular in England, at least among a certain section of society, before pattern books became widely available. The word sampler appears in the works of the Welsh poet, Tudur Aled, who died in 1520, as well as in the writings of his contemporary, John Skelton, who lived from about 1460 to 1529. Skelton's poetry reflects something of the life at Court, which he had seen at first hand, and he talks of samplers in a poem written around 1504 entitled 'Phyllyp Sparowe', as well as in his later long poem, 'Garlande of Laurell' (*c.* 1523). Describing the occupations of the ladies-in-waiting at the household of the Countess of Surrey, he writes:

> With that the tappettis and carpettis were layd,
> Whereon theis ladys softly myght rest,
> The saumpler to sow on, the lacis to enbraid;
> To weue in the stoule sume were full preste,
> With slaiss, with tauellis, with hedellis well drest.

Shakespeare evidently noticed women at work on samplers and he refers to the fashionable practice in two of his plays. In the bloody tragedy *Titus Andronicus* (*c.* 1590), Marcus recalls how Philomel had her tongue cut out by her sister's husband Tereus, so she could not reveal what he had done to her. But when Marcus encounters his ravished niece Lavinia with not only her tongue cut out but also her hands cut off, he exclaims:

> Fair Philomel, why she but lost her tongue,
> And in a tedious sampler sew'd her mind;
> But, lovely niece, that mean is cut from thee.
> A craftier Tereus, cousin, hast thou met,
> And he hath cut those pretty fingers off
> That could have better sew'd than Philomel.

Shakespeare's reference to Philomel using a sampler to recount her version of the cruel tragedy that had befallen her is interesting. Samplers generally did not contain accounts of events; even when inscriptions became popular in the mid-seventeenth century, the storytelling element was rare.

A few years later, in the comedy *A Midsummer Night's Dream*, Helena gently reminds Hermia:

> We, Hermia, like two artificial Gods,
> Have with our needles created both one flower,
> Both on one sampler, sitting on one cushion,
> Both warbling of one song, both in one key,
> As if our hands, our sides, voices and minds,
> Had been incorporate.

In order to understand when and how these early samplers were used, we must turn to one of the best contemporary accounts of this, found in a story by Barnabe Riche called *Of Phylotus and Emilia* (1581). Talking about the habits of a rich lady he says:

Now, when she had dined, then she might seke out her examplers, and to peruse whiche worke would doe beste in a ruffe, whiche in a gorget, whiche in a sleeve, whiche in a quaife, whiche in a caule, whiche in a handcarcheef; what lace would doe beste to edge it, what seame, what stitche, what cutte, what garde: and to sitte her doune and take it forthe by little and little, and thus with her nedle to passe the after noone with devising of thinges for her owne wearynge.

In spite of all this documentary evidence of early samplers, we have only a very few existing examples on which to base our ideas as to what sixteenth-century samplers actually looked like. Two of the earliest surviving specimens, one thought to be a German sampler for church linen, and the other Italian, are unfinished. They both contain a random assortment of motifs, probably collected over a long period of time. The

## Samplers

RIGHT Unfinished German sampler in coloured silks on linen. The crucifix was a fairly common motif in early sixteenth-century continental samplers; alphabets were less usual. The motifs resemble those in the earlier pattern books, and similar ones have been found on a piece of sixteenth-century German church linen in the Victoria and Albert Museum.

OPPOSITE Susan Nebabri's delicate band sampler, a forerunner of the style that was to become so popular in the seventeenth century.

## The Early Examples

German one, worked in cross stitch, long-armed cross, two-sided Italian cross and double running stitch, contains mostly geometric motifs but there are also some figures, a stylized tree and a crucifix, which is rare in English samplers at any time. The Italian piece, worked in back, satin and long-armed cross stitches, has many patterns for the embroidered borders which were so popular on household and personal linen.

A remarkable and exquisitely beautiful band sampler of cut and drawn threadwork with needlepoint fillings, believed to have been made in England around 1580–1600, is kept in the Museum of London. It measures 15 cm (6 in) across by 91.25 cm (36½ in) high and contains fifteen bands of different designs worked in silk, linen and metal threads on a linen ground. The top row of this delicate piece contains two large 'S' motifs either side of a rose, and is in red silk and gold thread. The fourth and widest band has 'E.R.' worked into it above the royal arms of Queen Elizabeth I, and below the crest the name of the worker, Susan Nebabri. Nothing is known about her, but her surname might suggest Spanish or Italian parentage. The other panels contain typical lace patterns including a fleur-de-lis and some birds, animals and flowers. Band samplers were probably popular at this time, though it is a style that is most often associated with the seventeenth century.

The earliest known sampler to be signed and dated was skilfully worked by Jane Bostocke, evidently as a gift to Alice Lee, then two years old. This sampler, discovered in 1960, differs from the others in several ways: apart from the added date, it has a squarish form and a relatively orderly arrangement.

The silks used are red, brown, green, blue and white with some metallic thread, pearls and beads on an unbleached linen ground. It is composed of spot motifs above, with both border and all-over patterns below. There is a small row of an acorn and oak-leaf band pattern, as well as carnation and geometric designs. The two types of grape and vine-leaf all-over patterns may contain a religious significance: the inhabited vine, with birds and animals feeding on the fruits, is a common motif in early Christian art because it is an image of the Christians feeding on the Eucharist. However, the popularity of the vine as a sampler motif did not last for more than a century or so.

History does not relate whether Alice Lee used this fine example of stitchery to make her own sampler, or indeed to make chair covers or wall hangings for her home. Had she done so, she would have been able to draw upon examples of back, satin, chain, ladder, buttonhole, detached buttonhole, cross, arrowhead, interlacing, pattern couching, coral and two-sided Italian cross stitches, with some speckling, bullion

and french knots. A fine array, indeed! The motifs include a chained bear, a deer, a dog, and a heraldic leopard as well as two trees and a squirrel. A castle has been traced from remaining stitch holes where the silk has rotted and is believed to have come from an unknown printed pattern as it was later reproduced in a nineteenth-century European sampler. Jane Bostocke's sampler also has an alphabet lacking a J, U and Z, as was common for the time.

Jane Bostocke was possibly an aunt or godmother to Alice Lee, but all she tells us in her inscription is:

ALICE : LEE : WAS : BORNE : THE  : 23 : OF NOVEMBER : BEING : TWESDAY : IN : THE : AFTER : NOONE : 1596

In many ways this piece is ahead of its time. Worked in the last years of England's Tudor age, its style and spirit more closely resemble the sophisticated tradition of sampler-making that would develop in the next hundred years.

OPPOSITE Jane Bostocke's gift sampler, worked in 1598, is the earliest known example to be both signed and dated.

# 2
# England's Golden Age

The seventeenth century produced some of the most beautiful samplers ever made, particularly in England. There were several different types, and many were still worked as reference and not intended for show. But almost all of them displayed exquisitely fine and varied stitchery combined with sophisticated designs and colour schemes; they were executed with an eye for detail, neatness and perfection. The period is often referred to as the golden age of sampler-making, for although the craft would thrive well into the nineteenth century it would, in England at any rate, lose much of its exuberance and originality.

England in the early 1600s was in a state of ferment; the established religious institutions were being challenged by increasing numbers among the population, and the accepted form of government was shortly to be attacked as well. There is scant evidence of this turmoil immediately visible in the samplers of the period, although references were occasionally made to historical events. By 1700, however, the growth of Puritanism and Protestant ideology had become clearly apparent in many of the verses which had begun to creep into samplers.

The roots of Puritanism are to be found in the reign of Queen Elizabeth I, and in particular in her failure to carry out reform of the English church along true Protestant lines. Elizabeth's *via media* between extreme Catholics and radical Protestants had failed to satisfy many of the eager religious exiles who had returned from Geneva and Zurich at the end of Mary's reign, and by the early seventeenth century this dissatisfaction had led to a unification, as Puritans, of most of the diverse Protestant groups.

When James I ascended the throne in 1603 his determination to emphasize the accepted Divine Right of Kings was bound to clash with the

OPPOSITE An English random sampler with a traditional thistle and rose pattern of the early seventeenth century, using silver thread and coloured silks on linen. Random or haphazardly worked samplers contained an impressively wide range of stitches.

corresponding new spirit in Parliament, as individual members were suddenly imbued with a new confidence, aggressiveness and sense of their own importance, often as a direct result of their Puritan beliefs. It was not long before Puritanism began to embrace many more than those opposed to the established Church: the word was politicized and used to describe anyone who defied the monarch's policies.

The new parliamentarians were not afraid to give voice to the grievances felt by a growing portion of early Stuart society; particularly volatile issues included the favouritism practised by James I and Charles I, the high rate of taxation, a trade monopoly enjoyed by the City of London, and the continued absence of Church reform. The Puritans claimed the religious justification of divine guidance for their actions, but they also reinforced their position by seeking legal precedents. Lawyers grew in number, and joined the broad spectrum of yeomen, artisans, gentlemen, ministers, merchants, and many others who found that Puritanism helped them make sense of their lives on earth and seemed to show them how best to enter the Heavenly Kingdom.

When Civil War finally broke out in 1642, members of the same economic classes found themselves on opposing sides, for the struggle was between an essentially despotic and centralizing system of government and the restraining powers of a more or less representative institution. England's social and economic equilibrium was never in any great danger; it was the political and constitutional situation which had prompted the crisis.

An important by-product of these tumultuous events was to cement the position and growing power of the middle classes. The same Puritan strength of purpose and self-reliance that had motivated Parliament informed the expansion of commerce and the growth of the professional ranks. This continued prosperity meant that, in general, the Elizabethan tradition of embroidery continued to flourish, at least during the first quarter of the seventeenth century. Needlework was also encouraged by the Protestant ethic, for it was thought to be a good way to banish idleness in young girls. The floral designs used for table covers, cushions and wall hangings were, if anything, bolder than in the sixteenth century, with many exotic blooms coming to the fore. Biblical scenes such as the sacrifice of Isaac, the story of Jonah and the Whale, and the Angel appearing to Sarah and Abraham, as well as figures personifying the Seasons and the Elements, were all much in vogue as needlework subjects. Towards the end of the century especially, animals became an extremely popular motif.

Embroidery pictures were much admired at this time and although some examples were worked for cushions or caskets, small book covers and mirror frames, others were intended simply as framed pictures. The caskets often depicted several scenes from an Old Testament story and would be used to hold small trinkets. They might be lined with silk with a mirror on the lid.

The techniques used for most of these items would often be the classic canvas stitch, tent stitch. But one type of work which became the height of fashion at this time was called stumpwork. This was a departure from Elizabethan traditions, but probably owed its origins to the raised and padded work that was widely seen in Elizabethan embroidery. Stumpwork started in the reign of James I and had a short-lived popularity, dying out by the 1680s. A three-dimensional type of work notable, according to some, for its realism but, according to others, for its grotesque ugliness, stumpwork was usually done on grounds of ivory-coloured satin enriched by the worker with silk and metallic threads, seed pearls and coloured beads. Its name derived from 'embroidery on the stump', a reference to the wooden stumps that were attached to the background material and used as the faces, arms and legs of the characters portrayed. The wood was generally closely covered with silk or satin, and costumes were well padded with wool. Sometimes facial features were painted on. The rest of the embroidered picture might be in long or short stitch, satin, split or tent stitch.

Another brief departure from Elizabethan styles was an attempted revival of ecclesiastical embroidery prompted by the attempts of Charles I's Archbishop Laud to reintroduce some of the traditional splendour and richness into church decoration. This was a controversial effort, to say the least, but no doubt some amateur needlewomen were inspired to produce their finest, most richly decorated work for the Church.

Neither the brief fashion for stumpwork nor that for church embroidery found its way on to the samplers of the age; some reasons for this will be examined later. Nevertheless many pieces – whether bed hangings, boxes, pictures, church furnishings or samplers – display a remarkable similarity of pattern, an indication that pattern books had become a more readily available source of designs.

One of the most popular seventeenth-century pattern books was *The Needle's Excellency*, printed for James Boler in 1631 'At The Signe of the Marigold in Paules Church Yard'. This contained many patterns from Johann Sibmacher's book of the previous century and it clearly seems to have been an instant success, passing rapidly into several editions. The title page of the book describes it as 'A New Booke wherin are divers Admirable Workes wrought with the Needle. Newly

invented and cut in Copper for the pleasure and profit of the Industrious'. Below this a picture of three women – Wisdome, Industrie, and Follie – points to the importance of embroidery for preventing idleness: Industrie has a piece of needlework in her hand.

The book was compiled by John Taylor, a man equally well known for his eccentric exploits on the waters as for his talents at making rhyming couplets. He styled himself 'the water poet' and prefaced the volume with the following poem called 'The Praise of the Needle':

> Let not opinion be preiudicate
> But mend it, ere they dare to discommend.
> So fare-thou-well my wel-deseruing Booke,
> (I meane, the workes deserts, and not my lines)
> I much presume that all that on it looke,
> Will like and laude the workemans good designes.
> Fooles play the fooles, but 'tis through want of wit,
> Whilst I to wisedomes censure doe submit.

Taylor said the patterns came:

> From the remotest part of Christendome
> Collected with much paines and industrie
> Thus are these workes farre fetch'd and dearly bought,
> And consequently good for ladyes thought.

He suggested the following stitches for them:

> For Tent-worke Rais'd-worke, Laid-worke, Frost-worke, Net-worke,
> Most curious Purles, or rare Italian cutworke,
> Fine Ferne-stitch, Finny-stitch, New-stitch and Chain-stitch,
> Braue Bred-stitch, Fisher-stitch, Irish-stitch and Queene-stitch,
> The Spanish-stitch, Rosemary-stitch, and Mowse-stitch,
> The smarting Whip-stitch, Back-stitch and the Crosse-stitch,
> All these are good and we must allow
> And these are everywhere in practise now.

Unfortunately, the names of many of these stitches have now passed into oblivion.

Surviving copies of this book are rare, no doubt because the easiest method of transferring the patterns from the printed page to the piece about to be worked was still by pouncing, which ultimately destroyed the paper.

Rivalling *The Needle's Excellency* in popularity was publisher Richard Shorleyker's *A Scholehouse for the Needle*, first produced in 1624. His book proclaimed that it contained:

> Certaine Patternes of Cut-workes: newly invented and never published before. Also sundry sortes of spots as Flowers, Birdes and fishes, etc. and will fitly serve to be wrought some with gould, some with silke, some with crewel in coullers: or otherwise at your pleasure.

Shorleyker also included a small section on how to enlarge or reduce a motif by using squared paper.

That both these books should insist that their patterns were newly invented gives some idea of the fierce competition engaged in by the publishers. The seventeenth century saw a flood of such works, all of which tried to satisfy the appetites of Stuart embroideresses for small creatures such as birds, caterpillars, frogs, butterflies, snails, flies and beetles as well as larger ones including peacocks, lions, rabbits, snakes, deer, swans and fish. Several of the motifs in both Shorleyker's book and *The Needle's Excellency* have been traced in many types of contemporary embroidery and samplers. Books intended for students of botany still doubled as sources of patterns for needlewomen, and gardening books were also sometimes used. Occasionally, pictorial designs drawn on linen and offered for sale at commercial workshops would be used by sampler-makers.

During the seventeenth century samplers were serving several purposes. In the early 1600s, at any rate, they were still worked by adult

OPPOSITE Lions and stags were among the most popular motifs for the English random samplers of the seventeenth century. Worked in coloured silks and metallic thread on linen, this portion of a sampler is an excellent example of the realistic shading shared by so many of the spot samplers.

35

An exquisite Italian sampler from the
seventeenth century, signed but not
dated, with cut- and drawnwork in
silver and white linen thread on linen,
and needlepoint filling. Italy was the
home of fine lacework; this sampler
may have been worked by a member
of Siena's Piccolomini family.

needlewomen as pattern records; on the whole these were composed of spot motifs arranged in a haphazard manner. They also remained a good means of practising a certain technique and the cut-, drawn- and lacework types might have been used for this. The most common seventeenth-century samplers comprised several rows of border patterns worked in coloured and white silks, often with bands of more complicated openwork at the bottom. Initially these too had been reference sheets, but increasingly they were made by younger children as a technical exercise, and soon they were being taught in schools.

The random or haphazardly worked samplers are often considered the liveliest, most colourful and imaginative kind ever made. It is clear from the needle marks on many of them, which indicate much unpicking, that they were frequently used as trial grounds for experimenting with designs. They consist of animal and flower motifs as well as small bursts of continuous, all-over patterns, and often employ silver and gold metallic thread, beads, pearls and sequins. It is possible that these motifs were used for applied work. They could be worked separately – with the sampler close at hand, no doubt, as the master pattern – and then cut out and applied to, for example, a velvet hanging. This was much easier than attempting to embroider directly on to such a rich material. But they were also used as patterns to be copied for making small items such as purses and pin cushions. A number of these, now in the Victoria and Albert Museum, contain motifs which are very similar to those on random samplers in the Museum collection.

Some of the flower, fruit and bird patterns were worked with highly realistic shading, a feature also seen to a lesser extent on band samplers of the time. Seventeenth-century needlewomen had no colour charts to assist them with shading and they were fond of colours of the brightest hues – predominantly blues, pinks, yellows, greens and rust. Lions and stags were probably the most popular animals represented, but there were also many small creatures such as caterpillars, snails and butterflies as well as the occasional fish, with grapes, strawberries, carnations and the Tudor rose among the favourite fruits and flowers. In fact, a very wide range of flora and fauna flourished on seventeenth-century sampler canvases.

People also played a part in random samplers. The earliest dated example of figures is on a random sampler of 1630, which shows a man and a woman, possibly the parents of the worker, holding hands. Below them are the initials CR for the reigning monarch, Charles I. The sampler is worked in silk and metallic threads on linen and contains flowers and animals as well as blocks of geometric patterns. From this decade

Worked in 1630, this Stuart piece is the earliest dated random sampler to contain human figures.

## Samplers

onwards figures are well represented on all types of seventeenth-century samplers, including the cut-, drawn- and lacework variety.

The specimen patches of all-over designs were mainly variations of diaper patterns, but also included snatches of stylized flowers; florentine work was very popular, too. The list of stitches used is enormous and includes some of the most complicated, such as plaited braid, which requires about five successive stages per stitch, guilloche, Russian overcast, rococo, Hungarian, Roumanian, Algerian eye, Montenegrin cross, tent, interlacing, double running, two-sided Italian cross and bullion knots. Laid and couched work are also seen on random samplers. Usually the motifs were arranged asymmetrically, with no eye for design, but occasionally the patterns were worked in neat, square blocks or diamonds more or less in rows. A remarkable and lavish early seventeenth-century sampler measuring $60 \times 21.25$ cm ($24 \times 8\frac{1}{2}$ in) has squares and rectangles of differing sizes containing a diversity of stitches in silver and silver-gilt thread with sequins and silk on linen. The blocks are all very tightly packed together with two of the squares containing crowns, below one of which are the initials IR (Iacobus Rex) for James I. The Victoria and Albert Museum, where this is kept, also has a pincushion worked with parts of exactly the same pattern.

A brief perusal through a batch of spot motif samplers makes it quite plain that fine craftmanship abounds. None the less, it seems certain that these pieces would have been rolled up and put away in a work basket to be consulted or added to when necessary throughout the worker's lifetime. And so it was natural that this kind of sampler was rarely signed or dated, although a few contained initials, sometimes the worker's and sometimes the monarch's, wherever there was a suitable space.

The best known of all seventeenth-century samplers are the band samplers. They, too, contain some very fine examples of delicate work and, in addition, they furnish us with some interesting information about social history. Generally, the bands are of border patterns sewn in coloured silks which would have been used on both costume and domestic linens. Sometimes there is a small selection of spot motifs above or below the bands. Other band samplers had the border patterns interspersed with the lines of a poem, although these are occasionally difficult to read since the last letter of a word would often start the next line; in one example the lines are upside down in relation to the patterns.

These samplers are almost all made on long narrow strips of linen. Length was probably decided by the maximum loom width of the day; 50 cm (20 in) is clearly average, as seen from contemporary valances and bedhangings, and was most popular for samplers. Some, however, were as long as 75 or 90 cm (30 or 36 in), and an exceptionally industrious worker might embroider a sampler that was as long as 105 cm (42 in) – but such keenness was rare! The width was probably the choice of the worker, who wanted just enough room for one large pattern or two and a half repeats of a smaller one, but not too much room so that working the same pattern became boring. Widths varied from 15 to 30 cm (6 to 12 in). Occasionally a double sampler was made with two 15-cm (6-in) panels alongside each other and a narrow 2.5-cm (1-in) strip down the centre which might contain an alphabet in a single colour. Most linen was still imported at this time and was very costly, so it is hardly surprising that one feature these samplers all have in common is extreme denseness, with hardly a space left unworked. The side edges were almost all hand-hemmed with selvedges top and bottom.

The coloured bands contained a huge variety of intricate patterns and stitches. There were geometrical and formal floral designs with the same carnations, roses, strawberries and pansies that are seen on the spot motif type worked into the border patterns. Sometimes pairs of birds made an attractive arrangement and one of the most popular motifs – worked sometimes in threesomes and sometimes in a double border pattern – was the acorn, with or without the oak leaves. The acorn is used with more variety than almost any other fruit or flower, and the oak leaf has played an important role in British mythology ever since the Druids held the oak tree in great veneration. In the seventeenth century the oak had a special significance for the Royalists after Charles II was said to have concealed himself in such a tree when fleeing from Oliver Cromwell and the Puritan Army during the Battle of Worcester in September 1651. From the mid-seventeenth century the pea flower with open pods was often turned into a stylized sampler border pattern as well as a spot motif. Its popularity may be due to the stylized patterns of pea pods included in Shorleyker's pattern book, or it may be that by this time the relatively new garden pea had become a common vegetable. Yet even when the pattern subjects on two or three samplers were similar, individual interpretations produced a variety of final effects.

At the beginning of the century outline patterns were the favourite method of execution, persisting from Elizabethan days. But gradually, a brighter, more solid effect was produced, chiefly by using satin stitch to fill in the outline. Detached buttonhole stitch was also much in vogue – the nearest seventeenth-century samplers came to stumpwork – and was used chiefly for rose petals on band samplers. This gave the bloom a most realistic effect of a double flower, mirroring the new fashions in garden roses. Sometimes each petal would be worked quite separately

OPPOSITE Nineteen rows make up this English band sampler worked by Elisabeth in 1629. The two figures carrying heart-shaped flowers at the top are 'boxers', a form that derived from the popular continental motif of a lover and his beloved exchanging gifts.

and sewn together later; another method was to work the petals in a circular fashion from a central point in the flower. In either case, they would be barely attached to the flower.

A strange feature of many of these band samplers is that one or more of the rows is often worked upside down. One explanation of this is that the symmetry of the pattern demanded it – but that is rarely the case. A more likely reason is that it allowed two friends, or sisters, perhaps, to work on a sampler together, sewing from opposing ends. The speech from *A Midsummer Night's Dream* referred to earlier, in which Helena talks of working on the same sampler as Hermia, seems to bear this out.

Many band samplers had one line reserved for two or three small male figures walking sideways, sometimes glancing over their shoulders, and carrying in one hand a small, unrecognizable object which could look like an acorn, a flower or spray, or be heart-shaped. They are often naked, worked only in outline, but occasionally they are clothed, either with rather 1920s-looking shorts and tops, and bobbed hairstyles, or with the costume of the day, which might include a tail coat and a long wig. These little figures have been the subject of much recent scholarship and have been given the name of 'boxers' by modern generations because of their pose with one leg forward and one arm up. (True boxers will be quick to point out that that stance would not win them many rounds in a fight!) It is clear, however, that the boxers derive from a motif that was frequently seen in continental Europe throughout the sixteenth and seventeenth centuries – that of two lovers exchanging gifts. In English samplers the female lover has clearly been transformed into a bush, or a tree, or just an unrecognizable shape with splay feet and possibly sprouting acorns. But usually a head, body, arms and legs are dimly recognizable and the lover offers his sprig of foliage – the love trophy – to this being.

Other types of bands included the ancient 'S' motif, which was usually slanting and joined with bars across the middle. This motif naturally had special significance for the House of Stuart. One or two rows were frequently taken up by a technique known as Assisi work, originating from the town in Northern Italy, where the patterns were worked in reverse by stitching only the background to reveal a picture area that was left blank. The designs for Assisi work were often heraldic, with only one colour used, to give a formal, dignified look.

Many of these band samplers contained cut-, drawn- and lacework at the bottom, while others were composed entirely of rows of open-work, perhaps with the addition of some whitework embroidery.

At the top of her sampler, Ann Edwards had room for just one large flower, so she filled in the surrounding area of the band with a stag, birds and a duck. She worked her name and the date, 1706, upside down at the very top.

## Samplers

Mierevelt's 'A Dutch Lady', 1628. Fulsome ruffs with finely worked lace edging were popular throughout aristocratic circles in the first half of the seventeenth century, and the designs for them are the same as those seen in many contemporary samplers.

Generally, this latter type displayed a perfection of minute execution, but it must also have been the most painstaking kind of sampler to produce, probably taking many months to complete, and requiring more patience than most young girls could muster.

The lavishness of Court costume during the reign of James I meant that the demand for lace was still extremely high, especially as edging for ruffs. But as this kind of fancy ruff might have required approximately 22.5 metres (25 yards) of finely worked lace it may be assumed that it would have been a product of professional lacemakers only! The lace patterns in samplers were most likely used for smaller items of clothing such as baby caps, night caps, cuffs, handkerchiefs and cravats (widely worn by both men and women at the time), as well as for edging on household linens. It is interesting that even during the Cromwellian Protectorate, when simplicity was the order of the day and fancy lace additions to clothing were theoretically taboo, lace patterns continued to appear in samplers. In fact, the cut- and drawnwork only began seriously to decline once lace imports reached Britain in significant amounts towards the end of the century. And some kinds of needlepoint lacework remained popular even then.

Nearly all openwork samplers consisted of border patterns and single motifs taken primarily from the books of pattern suggestions. Many of them appeared on the coloured band samplers too. Mostly worked in linen thread on linen, there were two main techniques. In the first case, both warp and woof threads were removed, except possibly for a few connecting bars or, if the pattern demanded, diagonal bars would be sewn in. In the second, just one set of threads, either horizontal or vertical, was removed. The first type is most like needlepoint lace and is seen in some of the finest and earliest samplers of the century. The designs are built up first by overcasting the raw edges which have been cut, then by rows of buttonholing, with each row being worked into the previous one. The second type is most like the drawn threadwork which is still in popular use today as edging for goods such as tray cloths or handkerchiefs. Another type of drawn threadwork created a pattern by interlacing threads first around the overcast bars, which made up several small squares, and then across the squares. This method was as popular as the cutwork with needlepoint stitches, but not quite as delicate.

One of the most beautiful cutwork samplers was made in 1649 and signed SID, with the initials AI, perhaps a teacher, appearing to the right of that below the date. The initials are in lacework, an unusual feature at that time. Using rows of buttonholing technique, the first band of this white sampler shows the Angel appearing to Sarah and Abraham

Cutwork sampler signed SID, 1649. Strictly speaking, cutwork (or openwork), where the pattern is made by taking away from the background material rather than by embellishing the existing cloth, is not embroidery. This intricately worked piece includes not only cutwork, but also delicate detached buttonhole stitches.

## Samplers

by a pavilion with an opened curtain detached from the ground. Sarah, who is holding up her hand in astonishment at the Angel's announcement, is clothed in a headdress, collar and skirt, all in relief; the skirt is sewn with very tiny fleur-de-lis. These detached pieces are often seen in elaborate samplers; in some cases the lace has been worked quite separately and sewn on later. Other lines worked by SID include the 'S' motif, roses and tulips, the acorn, a veiled mermaid and some peapods, open and full of peas. It is quite possible that the Abraham and Sarah motif came from a pattern book, as an almost exact replica of this scene exists on another, much smaller openwork sampler. In the second sampler, which is undated and unsigned, the only other row also contains an Angel, this time with a flaming sword, appearing to Adam and Eve.

There is another English specimen, undated but believed to be from the second half of the seventeenth century, which contains a lacework alphabet, missing a few letters and spread over three rows. The similarity between these letters and those used by SID suggests that both could have been reproduced from a pattern book; Giovanni Ostau's of 1561 is thought to be the most likely one.

That many of these openwork samplers were intended as pattern records is clear because they were often left unfinished with the design in various stages of working. One mid-seventeenth-century sampler still has its original vellum tacked to the back of the top line of cutwork. This shows how the linen was held rigid after the threads were withdrawn and the pattern was built up. Most included several different techniques within the one piece, and were often completed with some rows of whitework. The most popular stitch for this was block satin in linen or silk thread, used to create geometric designs.

Judging by just one sampler, Margaret May must be counted as one of the most enthusiastic of seventeenth-century sampler-makers. Her piece, made in 1654, measured $73.75 \times 22.5$ cm ($29\frac{1}{2} \times 9$ in) and included examples of cut and drawn threadwork with needlepoint fillings, needle weaving and eyelet holes with satin, hem, double running, Russian drawn, and overcast filling stitches. Her whitework contained examples of geometric and stylized floral patterns. Although almost all of these open- and whitework samplers were in white only, one unsigned mid-century example has royal-blue beads scattered on several bands.

Towards the end of the century, rows of alphabets and numerals were being included in almost every band sampler. This fashion is a telling sign of increasing prosperity among the families of sampler-makers: it indicates that several sets of linen were now owned by many people, and that these valuable commodities needed both marking and numbering

Vellum was tacked to the back of a sampler in order to support the band about to be worked. It was generally used for more delicate pieces, and can be seen here still attached to the top row.

Needlework assumed the same importance in a girl's education as reading and writing. In this German print of *c.* 1700, the girl's mother looks on as she receives instruction from her teacher.

to enable the lady of the house to keep a constant check on her supplies of household napery. But the alphabets went hand in hand with the growing fashion for signatures at the bottom of samplers as well as short inscriptions. Together with the exceptional neatness of many pieces, where the back is almost indistinguishable from the front, these developments are a certain sign that samplers were slowly entering the realms of school exercises.

Samplers appear to have been taught in schools from quite early on in the century, for in 1639 playwright Jasper Mayne wrote in *The Citye Match*:

> Your schoole Mistresse that can expound and teaches
> To knit in Chaldee and worke Hebrew Samplers.

The introduction of alphabets and verses signalled a significant change in the primary function of the sampler. No longer just a record of stitches and patterns, from the mid-seventeenth century samplers also became a means of instilling moral values.

## Samplers

Initially, no doubt, the school samplers were used to familiarize young children with various embroidery and lacework techniques, and their form must owe something to the older idea of a sampler as a pattern record useful throughout life. One explanation for the openwork usually falling at the bottom of a coloured band sampler might be that it was probably not attempted until the young worker had mastered the simpler embroidery patterns. But from about 1650 onwards, the introduction of religious and moral inscriptions tells us that the use of a sampler as a pattern record was quickly becoming a secondary consideration. The real clue as to the change in function of the sampler is contained in the dates, signatures, and ages of the workers, all of which start appearing on samplers regularly from this time. Initials have been seen on samplers from an early date, but now full names are rarely omitted, sometimes with the initials included in another part of the work. An adult needleworker would only rarely sign a practice piece of work such as this, perhaps bowing to the fashion.

One of the most touching inscriptions is to be found on an undated and unsigned long band sampler of coloured silks on linen. In between the rows of fine embroidery the worker says:

> When I was young I little thought
> That wit must be so dearly bought
> But now experience tells me how
> If I would thrive then I must bow
> And bend unto another's will That
> I might learn both art and skill To
> Get My Living With My
> Hands That So I M
> ight Be Free From Ba
> nd And My Own Dam
> e that I may be And free from all suc
> h slavery. Avoid vaine pastime fle
> youthfull pleasure Let moderatio
> n allways be thy measure And so pr
> osed unto the heavenly treasure.

One wonders what sort of hardship this poor girl had experienced to make her express so fierce a longing for independence. The rhyme may, of course, have been a favourite of the 'dame' which she had given to her young charges to embroider as an object lesson in life.

In 1651 Martha Salter inscribed the bottom of her sampler with the words 'The feare of God is an excellent gift'. Four years later Ann Fenn used the rhyming couplet that was later to become so beloved:

46

> Ann Fenn is my name and with
> my hand I made the same.

There were many variations on this theme.

It is not long before we find the names of teachers also appearing in the inscriptions. For example:

> Mary Wright is M(y)
> NAME AND WITH my NE
> DL I wrought the sa
> me and Gooddy Readd wa
> s my dame 1669.

It is not clear whether Gooddy Readd and other specifically named teachers were private family instructors or school mistresses. It is rare for more than one sampler to mention the same teacher's name, even though in a number of the schools the teacher, rather than the pattern books, was probably the source of inspiration for a number of similarly designed samplers.

Mary Hall was one of the earliest young sampler workers to tell the world her age. She signed her piece: 'Mary Hall is my name and when I was thirteen years of age I ended this in 1662'. It seems that ten or eleven was the average age of sampler-makers at this time, although some eight-year-olds were also making them.

Both Martha Salter and Ann Fenn included alphabets in their samplers, a clue as to their being schoolwork pieces. In 1695 Elizabeth Eyls wrote: 'Schools are the seedplots of all learned arts, and doth enrich our heads our tongues our hearts.' Elizabeth must indeed have been an enthusiastic scholar, captivated by the new emphasis on school instruction that characterized the latter half of this period.

It was also in the late seventeenth century that children first acknowledged a debt of gratitude to their parents on a sampler. A smallish piece by Margreet Lucus in 1681, of coloured silk border patterns and some rows of whitework, has the following inscription at the bottom, followed by five rows of alphabet:

> My father hitherto hath done his best to make
> me a workewoman above the rest. Margreet
> Lucuh 1681 bezng ten year old come July the first.

The inclusion of alphabets and names, however, does not automatically mean that the worker was a schoolchild. Elizabeth Mackett's piece, measuring 108.75 × 18.75 cm (43½ × 7½ in), is executed in such an exquisitely proficient manner that it seems almost certain she was an adult

Part of Elizabeth Mackett's industrious band sampler, completed in 1696. The date, together with a second signature, appears after five further lines of whitework and four panels of cutwork and another alphabet.

## Samplers

needlewoman. She included ten rows of coloured silk border patterns, two rows of alphabets, eight lines of whitework and four panels of cutwork before signing off with another alphabet, this time in eyelet stitch, then her name and the date, 1696.

As late as 1675 Thomas Brooks wrote in *Paradise Opened*: 'Such as begin to work with the needle look much on their sampler and pattern: it is so in learning to write and indeed in learning to live also.' Evidently, the sampler had not yet totally lost its original function.

The work of one child, Martha Edlin, born in 1660, has a special place in sampler history since several pieces she embroidered have survived. In fact, it is likely that in the seventeenth century many children, from about the age of eight or nine onwards, would have progressed in the way that Martha did, making first a coloured silk sampler, then a lace- and whitework sampler, then an embroidered casket and finally, possibly, a stump- and beadwork picture.

Martha Edlin completed and signed her coloured band sampler in 1668. One year later her sampler of whitework and cut and drawn lace patterns, worked on a yellowish piece of linen with white linen thread, was finished, signed and dated, 16 ME 69. These samplers both include

Martha Edlin's richly embroidered work box, (1671) with, on the left, her coloured band sampler (1668) and, on the right, her sampler of cut and drawn lace patterns and whitework (1669). The samplers would have been rolled up and kept for reference in the work box, which was embroidered with stumpwork figures and raised work.

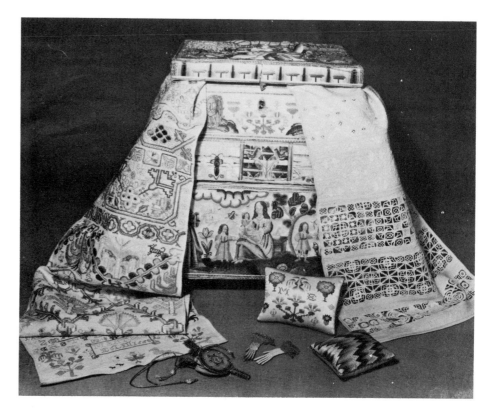

designs which have been traced to sixteenth-century pattern books and perpetuated in such publications as *The Needle's Excellency*. It took Martha just two more years to complete her richly embroidered cabinet, worked with seed pearls on the front panel and including stump- and raised work. This featured the Seven Virtues. Music and the Four Elements and was finished in 1671. Martha made various other small embroidery pieces and pincushions, which have been preserved together inside the box along with a set of silver toys. It may be assumed that industry and ability such as hers would have been rewarded by such toys. In 1673 Martha completed her final piece – a beadwork jewel box in which the beads are sewn on to a satin ground.

It is rare to find samplers used as commemorative pieces before the twentieth century, but one or two seventeenth-century examples are known which do record events and were probably inspired by teachers. In 1693 Martha Wright included the following inscription on a sampler:

the Prince of Orang landed in the West of England on the 5th of November 1688, and on the 11th April 1689 was crowned King of England, and in the year 1692 the French came to invade England, and a fleet of ships sent by King William, drove them from the English seas, and took, sunk, and burned twenty-one of their ships.

It was signed Martha Wright, 26 March 1693. The following year Mary Minshull embroidered an inscription below two rows of alphabet:

> THERE WAS AN EARTHQUAKE
> ON THE 8 OF SEPTEMBER 1692
> IN THE CITY OF LONDON
> BUT NO HURT THO IT
> CAUSED MOST PART
> OF ENGLAND TO
> TREMBLE

By the second half of the century many of the border patterns had become far too elaborate in both method and colour to be of great practical use in household decoration, especially when compared with the stunningly simple blackwork so popular in the sixteenth century. Evidently most seventeenth-century teachers were highly accomplished needlewomen with an enormous repertoire of stitches and techniques at their fingertips. Generally, the style of samplers was becoming out of touch with contemporary needlework styles. This disparity is most clearly seen with stumpwork. Nothing was quite so fashionable as this method, yet nowhere does it appear on samplers. This could, of course, be attributable to the fact that stumpwork made for a bulky and some-

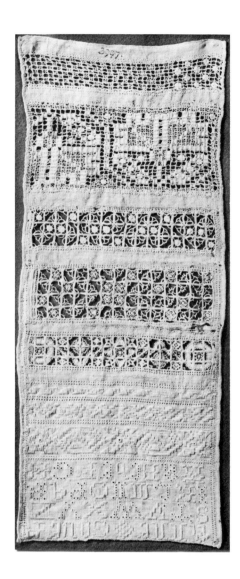

## Samplers

what fragile finished product, which did not lend itself easily to being rolled up and put away. But it is also possible that school teachers did not consider it a necessary part of a basic training in embroidery.

Similarly, crewelwork was, by mid-century, being used for bed hangings more often than canvas work or applied work. Crewel was mentioned by Shorleyker in his introduction in 1630, but it is not found in samplers of the time. Perhaps this too reflects a teacher's decision.

Seventeenth-century American samplers were almost indistinguishable from their English counterparts in terms of style, technique and design. The early colonists still looked very much to the mother country to set the fashion and to provide their supplies of cloth and thread. However, most of those that have survived are interesting more because of the personalities that shaped them than their original stitchery.

One or two notable samplers now housed in American museums are known to have crossed the Atlantic with the early settlers. They were able to take relatively few possessions with them on board ship and so a sampler, being not only small but also a cherished possession which might have many uses in the future, was one that few young women would choose to leave behind.

One of these was made by Anne Gower (or Gover according to her sampler) the first wife of Governor John Endecott. They arrived at Salem, Massachusetts, in 1628, and she died one year later. Her sampler of cut- and drawnwork, headed by several rows of whitework, although undated, is generally considered the earliest known in America. The top row contains her name and beneath that are three rows of the alphabet, worked in reverse order, in satin and eyelet stitch. If, as suspected, she made this during her childhood in about 1610, it is an early example both of a signature and an alphabet. It is also very fine work for such young hands.

The earliest sampler thought to have been made on American soil was by Loara Standish, who was born in 1623 and died in 1656. Her sampler was probably made around 1633, or at any rate when she was fairly young. Loara was the daughter of the famous Myles Standish, who was born in England, became a soldier in the Netherlands, and then sailed with the Pilgrim Fathers in the *Mayflower* in 1620. He soon became the captain, or military defender, of New Plymouth. As a soldier and a linguist he was invaluable for dealing with the Indian natives. The Standish sampler is fine needlework in the traditional English style of coloured threads in an intricate pattern. It also includes the following verse and is possibly in this respect the first of its kind:

> Loara Standish is My Name
> Lord Guide my Hart that I may do Thy Will
> Also Fill my hands with such convenient Skill
> As may conduce to Virtue void of Shame
> And I will give the Glory to Thy Name.

It is clear that young Loara, and no doubt many others like her, were from the very first as well-schooled in religion as in embroidery.

A sampler dated 1654, which was probably made in America, is extremely unusual in that it bears the names of a couple, Miles and Abigail Fleetwood, from which it may be assumed that the piece was worked after marriage. It contains the inscription:

> Miles Fletwod Abigail Fletwod 1654
> In prosperity friends will be plenty
> But in adversity not one in twenty.

which is generally taken to refer to Miles Fleetwood's unfortunate experiences with Oliver Cromwell's army. Tradition has it that Miles was a royalist while his brother was a member of Cromwell's forces.

Another early American sampler was made by Mary Hollingsworth (or Hollingworth according to her own spelling), probably around 1665. This was a typical seventeenth-century band sampler in coloured silks with stylized flower borders. According to a descendant, Mary intended it as a sampler of designs from which to work shawl borders, with the square figures at the top to be worked on the corners of the shawl.

On 1 July 1676 Mary married Philip English, the most prosperous merchant in the Salem area. However during an outbreak of witch-hunting hysteria in Salem suspicion fell on the couple, chiefly because they were Episcopalians – precisely the kind of persecution many Puritans had left England to avoid. Mary and Philip escaped to New York and returned only after the hysteria had died down. But the ordeal proved too much for Mary's health; she died in 1694, shortly after her return.

The seriousness of purpose which is at the very heart of sampler-making was bound to appeal to the solid, upright, Puritan families that chose New England as a place were they would have the necessary freedom to pursue the way of life in which they so passionately believed. It was not until the eighteenth century that inscriptions and verses would become an increasingly important part of samplers in America but, when they did, Protestant moralities coupled with the industriousness implicit in sampler-making, helped the craft to put down roots of its own in the new land. The individuality and spontaneity so characteristic of later American samplers will be examined in chapter four.

OPPOSITE Anne Clowser's Lord's Prayer (1723) is worked in silver thread and coloured silks on a woollen canvas. Setting an oval within a square was not a common practice, and the combination of the design and the delicate reds and greens of the floral surround provides a stunning and memorable sampler. The prominence of the border is unusual for an English piece.

ABCDEF G HIKLMMNOPQRSTVWX YZ X

THE LORDS PRA... | IS TIME TO EFCTNN
OUR FATHER WICh | THE TEN COMMandments
...HEAVEN ART TO | THOV SHALL HAVE NO OTHER
TO HALLOWD BE | GODS BVT ME NOT TO
THY NAME THYKI | NO IMAGE BOW THY
GDOM CO ME TH | KNEE TAKE NOT THE
WILL BE DONE II | NAME OF GOD IN VA
...EARTH EVEN AS TH | IN DO NOT THE SABB
SAME IN HEAVEN Is | ATH DAY PROFANE H
GIVE VS O LORD | ONOVT THY FATHER AND MOTHER
OVT DAILY BREAD | TOO AND SEE THAT THOU NO MU
THIS DAY AS WE | THER DO FROM VILE ADVLTTY KE
FORGIVE OVR DE | EP THEE CLEAN STEAL NOT ALTHO
BTORS SO FORGIve | VGH THY STATE BE MEAN FALSS
OUT DEBTS WE PT... | WITNESS BEAT THOU
...NO TEMPTATION | NOT OF THAT WHICh
LEAD VS NOT FTOm | IS THY NEIGHBOUTS
EVIL KEEP US FREE | DO NOT COVET X X
FOT KINGDOM PO | DOROHY
WET AND GLORY | CRAME xxMET

SAMPLET x1734

# 3

# The Schoolroom Products

The first few decades of the eighteenth century brought to England greater stability than the country had known for hundreds of years. A desire for power, profit and status had become a far more important guiding motive for many Englishmen than fighting over rights and privileges, and there emerged an essentially self-satisfied and materialistic society that was tired of wars, rebellions and unheavals. The interests of mercantile and landed wealth coalesced into one oligarchy, and a fundamental political stability cemented the old social equilibrium. Men of new wealth were appearing, too, in the small towns with young industries and, whatever their background, could there achieve social and political power at a lower level with much greater ease than if England had been a more complex and industrially advanced society. Generally, after 1715, they too became part of this oligarchy; there was a common sense of identity between those who wielded political, social and economic control. The core of the system was the hearty, robust, epicurean, Sir Robert Walpole, Prime Minister for so much of the century. A genuine connoisseur of the visual arts, his sense of humour, encouragement of trade and religious toleration, albeit with anti-Catholic leanings, were qualities mirrored by many among the ruling classes at the time.

During his spell in power, and indeed throughout the century, there was a noticeable increase in the number of rich farmers and industrialists, often self-made men, whose social pretensions led them and their wives to cultivate a 'drawing-room existence' in an effort to prove they were gentlemen and ladies. The need to educate children, including the girls, in certain subjects, was recognized more clearly than ever. And while needlework was still considered an essential part of any girl's education it could now, through the medium of a sampler, be combined with

OPPOSITE With The Lord's Prayer, a rhyming version of the Ten Commandments, both geometric and floral border patterns, an alphabet, a name and a date, Dorothy Greame's piece epitomizes the educational sampler produced in many schools throughout Britain in the eighteenth century.

RIGHT Moorland's 'Visit to the
Boarding School' shows the
importance placed on embroidery in
the curriculum. Two samplers hang
on the walls, while a teacher discusses
a particular pupil's needlework with
her mother.

BELOW 'Farmer Giles and his wife
showing off their daughter Betty to
their Neighbours on her return from
School'. Gillray's 1809 cartoon gently
satirizes the ethic of the rising middle
classes – and daughter Betty's sampler
has been given pride of place on the
parlour wall.

religious instruction, geography, mathematics, English literature and grammar. When completed, the sampler would be hung on the wall by proud parents as a record of achievement. It was a sign of belonging in the sturdy, upper-middle-class world.

Many of the samplers at this time had an air of drudgery about them associated with the schoolroom, but the same cannot be said for embroidery in general. From the late 1600s onwards this was often influenced by oriental patterns and designs, giving a new liveliness to old colour schemes and a touch of exotic flavour to the subject matter. A few surviving crewelwork coverlets and hangings with small oriental scenes including trees, rocks, pavilions, pagodas and bridges worked in brightly coloured silks are evidence of the way in which textiles imported from China, India and Persia influenced needlework fashions.

Crewelwork was one of the most popular types of handwork in eighteenth-century England, and was used for jackets, dresses and waistcoats as well as for bed covers, valances and hangings. But many silk embroidered coverlets were also made, often worked entirely in chain stitch, a technique derived from Indian embroidery. By mid-century, chain stitch was usually worked with a small hook instead of a needle, which drew a loop of thread from below the fabric to the surface. Reinserting the hook and repeating the steps produced a chain stitch much more quickly than the traditional needle. This method, called tambour work, is said to have been introduced into Europe in the late 1760s from India or China, where it was probably worked without a frame. But the French stretched the material to be embroidered in this way over a round frame, rather like the top of a drum (tambour), thus giving it its name.

The new printed textiles meant that the need for embroidered household items diminished slightly at this time. But professional draughtsmen, who frequently advertised their services, were much in demand as the source of new designs. There is one account of a Sussex schoolmaster-cum-draughtsman, Walter Gale, measuring out a hop garden for a Mr Baker in 1751 as well as drawing embroidery patterns for Mr Baker's daughters. There also existed many books of flower engravings where the clear outlines were often intended to help embroideresses and, towards the end of the century, embroidery patterns began to appear in publications such as the *Lady's Magazine* of the early 1760s. As yet, these were a mere trickle compared with the flood of such patterns that was to characterize the next century.

Knotting and quilting were other fashionable handicrafts in the early eighteenth century. In the former, ladies would make a series of knots

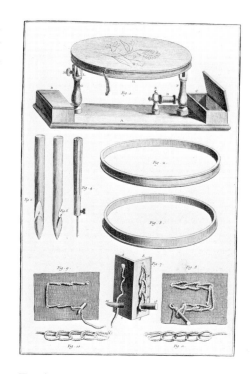

Tambour work took its name from the round frames over which the material to be embroidered was stretched.

in linen threads of various thicknesses by means of a shuttle. The finished knotting was then couched down to the background material, often creating a highly elaborate pattern which might be used for chair seats or bedcovers. Quilting involved outlining motifs with parallel lines of backstitching worked through two layers of material with linen padding between.

After about 1770 canvas work declined in favour and from then on there was a general deterioration in embroidery standards. Nowhere is this deterioration more visible than in contemporary samplers, which almost from the beginning of the eighteenth century ceased to be records of fine stitchery and elaborate designs or trial grounds for difficult techniques. Generally, they were now specimens of a young child's ability to work basic stitchery neatly and tidily. According to the eighteenth-century dictionary definition by Samuel Johnson, a sampler was '... a piece worked by young girls for improvement'.

In order to look suitable in a frame, the samplers became squarer. The usual size was about 32.5–45 cm (13–18 in) long and about 25–32.5 cm (10–13 in) wide, with a stylized border surrounding a verse and a few symmetrically arranged motifs of birds, flowers and trees. These were often in pairs, and, in comparison with the seventeenth-century type, were rather sparsely spread around the square of material. The need for economy had apparently vanished. The vast majority were made in schools and so alphabets and numerals were the order of the day. As the age of sampler workers dropped – often we find six-year-olds making them – it was inevitable that they were no longer such a formidable technical exercise. Nor is it surprising that many of the new embroidery techniques did not find their way on to samplers. But there are still sparks of vitality and originality shown and many young children portrayed their homes and parents in a way that is immensely touching and refreshing. Although their repertoire of stitches was small, those they knew how to use were executed proficiently.

The band sampler did not die away immediately, but already in the first part of the century it is possible to notice a slight effect on sampler design of the new printed cottons imported from India. The result was often brighter coloured samplers and some naturalistic floral patterns with curving instead of angular lines as in the band sampler border patterns. These patterns would often first be drawn freehand and one flower might be different from the next.

Linen was no longer the only material used for samplers. A rather yellowish, coarse-textured linen was fashionable for a few years at the beginning of the century, but by mid-century most samplers were worked on a fine woollen cloth called tammy. But this type of fabric was susceptible to moth damage and did not remain in favour for long. It normally had a loom width of 32.5 cm (13 in) and is recognizable by blue threads in the selvedge. Cotton is known to have been used for one or two samplers in the 1790s and satin was a favourite for maps, especially those with commercially drawn or printed outlines. But many of the map, and darning samplers were made on tiffany, a fine, muslin-like material. By the end of the century, linen, once again, was the preferred background fabric.

The most popular threads were still silk and linen; metallic thread was very rarely used. Innovations included chenille, which was popular on some map samplers, and human hair, which added a certain touch of sentimentality to a religious or moralizing verse, as in the following example:

Heavenly Love

Christ's Arms Do Still Stand Open To Receive
All weary Prodigals That Sin Do Leave
For Them He Left His Father's Blest Abode
Made Son of Man To Make Man Son Of God
To cure Their wounds He Lives Elixier bled
And Died A Death To Rise Them from The Dead.
This Work Was Done With The Hair of Mr Thomas Vickery
By Elizabeth, His Daughter, 1782.

The use of black silk for the verse was another means of emphasizing the poignancy of a sampler, especially one dedicated to a departed relative. Sometimes the satin maps were also embroidered in black only, but this was more in an effort to copy the effect of an engraving.

The choice of patterns and motifs on eighteenth-century samplers was influenced chiefly by the individual teacher who by this time, no doubt, had a store of favourite patterns that was passed on from one year to the next. Several motifs can still be traced to the sixteenth- and seventeenth-century pattern books; some of these patterns had undergone considerable metamorphoses, but others remained virtually unchanged.

One book whose patterns were reproduced in hundreds of samplers was John Brightland's *Grammar of the Englishe Tonge*, published in 1711. This contained an alphabet of capital letters, called sampler letters, which proved a boon for many a schoolteacher as several rows of alphabet were invariably included on one sampler. These were mostly worked in satin, eyelet or cross stitch. Both lower case and capital letters were embroidered in differing sizes, sometimes with an example of each together. Occasionally the alphabet was worked in reverse order; at other times, the end of a row was reached with a few letters still unworked, and these would be jettisoned. In order to ensure that the letters would fit exactly into one line, they were sometimes arranged in triangles, as below. Numerals might also be incorporated:

|   | B |   | E |   | H |   | K |   | N |   | Q |   | T |   | W |   | A |
|---|---|---|---|---|---|---|---|---|---|---|---|---|---|---|---|---|---|
| A | C | D | F | G | I | J | L | M | O | P | R | S | U | V | X | Y | Z |
|   | 1 |   | 2 |   | 3 |   | 4 |   | 5 |   | 6 |   | 7 |   | 8 |   | 9 |

In the early part of the century such a pattern would have been organized without the letters J, U and Z. One means of completing a row after the end of the alphabet was to include digits from 0 to 9. Rows of double figures might also be worked. Sometimes flourishes in double running stitch were added to eighteenth-century alphabets, a feature especially popular in Scottish samplers.

Perhaps some children learned the alphabet through stitching the letters on a sampler but clearly others were already quite familiar with it by the time they first worked one. We do know that the task of sampler-making was increasingly associated with very young members of a school, as Oliver Goldsmith observed. In *She Stoops to Conquer*, written in 1773, Hastings comments, 'For instance, miss there, would be considered as a child, a mere maker of samplers.'

There are a few surviving specimens of samplers made by young boys around this time. This can probably be explained by the informal nature of many small village schools where, at times, the boys would have to do whatever the girls were doing. Some of the boys' samplers also included other names, which might indicate that they were made in conjunction with other members of the family. A 1762 piece, which is squarish and bordered but made in the floral band fashion of the previous century, concludes with the verse:

> Immortal made what Should We Mind
> So Much As Immortality
> Of beings for A Heaven Designed
> What but A Heaven the Care should be.

This is signed Robert Henderson in black silk, with Jean and Christan Henderson and the year 1762 alongside. Two others by boys which have been recorded include one signed Lindsay Duncan Cuper, 1788, and another with the inscription: 'Mathew was born on April 16, 1764, and sewed this in August, 1774.' A sampler worked in 1795, with the names

Andrew Brunnell and Elizabeth Brunnell, both surrounded by a garland of flowers, contains an East View of the Liverpool Lighthouse and Signals on Bidston Hill. Certainly a boy's subject, but perhaps his sister helped him work it.

The inclusion of a border is one of the major features distinguishing eighteenth-century samplers from their predecessors. Initially, just a fraction of a border might have been included to fill in space on either side of a panel, and, as such, it was a fairly logical development of a band sampler. But gradually, from 1720 onwards, as the decorative potential of the border was grasped, three and then four sides of the sampler were surrounded. A good example of how this came about is a sampler by Susanna Wilkinson, dated 1699–1700, which is in many ways a transitional piece. Her first two rows are quite ordinary satin stitch band patterns followed by seven rows of alphabets and numerals, typical of the schoolgirl exercise. However, she followed this with some very proficient examples of cutwork, popular a century earlier, and point lace insertions which she used to depict two figures. These are believed to have been copied from portraits of James I and his wife. On either side of them is a simple border in red silk.

One of the earliest border designs used was a pattern of trefoils, but stylized flowers and geometric patterns, often rather thin and boring, quickly became the almost universally accepted border design. Ann Clowser's exquisitely beautiful sampler of 1723 was a most original piece. Made with silver thread and mostly pink and green silks on wool, she embroidered the Creed and The Lord's Prayer within an oval tablet in the centre of her work. She surrounded the words with a naturalistic border of flowing leaves and flowers, which is the main focal point of the whole piece, and then squared it off with a border of florentine work. The style of the floral border was obviously influenced by printed oriental designs and their imitation in crewelwork; in fact the total effect is more reminiscent of a quilt than a sampler.

Anne Haskins was another early embroideress to set off the beautiful design of her sampler with a border. She worked panels of stylized flowers, a row of fleur-de-lis and an alphabet followed by the Creed; below this she embroidered a country house, set in a park with animals, trees and flowers. Two thick, vertical bands of finely worked florentine stitch bordered the whole scene. This sampler is dated 9 October 1732.

Although the choice of border was probably decided by the schoolmistress, many of the most popular styles were those with age-old symbolic meanings. It is doubtful if the countless thousands of children who embroidered these motifs and patterns were ever aware of their

Surviving samplers worked by boys are rare. This nineteenth-century example with its touching verse is very simple, but is well worked and neatly designed for one so young.

The inclusion of complete scenes on samplers gained in popularity during the eighteenth century, and their decorative nature provided a contrast to the obligatory verses. Anne Haskins worked this piece in 1732.

deeper meanings. One of the easiest to recognize is the trefoil, often transformed into trilobe-shaped flowers symbolizing the Holy Trinity. Sometimes this is represented by three flowers on one stem or three sprays in one vase. A flower which lends itself particularly well to this idea is the tri-coloured pansy, a much-loved sampler flower. One of its common names is *Herba Trinitatis*, which gives a clear indication of its religious significance.

Perhaps the favourite – or indeed, the most hackneyed – of all sampler border patterns was the strawberry. The attraction lay partly in its distinctive shape and the contrast of its red fruit and green leaves, but the strawberry also had religious connotations. Having neither thorns

The sampler text (embroidered) reads:

When I can read my title clear.  
To mansions in the skies.  
I bid farewell to every fear,  
And wipe my weeping eyes.

Should earth against my soul engage.  
And hellish darts be hurl'd.  
Then I can smile at Satan's rage.  
And face a frowning world.

Let cares like a wild deluge come.  
And storms of sorrow fall.  
May I but safely reach my home.  
My God. my heav'n. my all.

There shall I bathe my weary soul.  
In seas of heav'nly rest.  
And not a wave of trouble roll.  
Across my peaceful breast.

Far from my thoughts vain world begone  
Let my religious hours alone.  
Fain would my eyes my Saviour see.  
I wait a visit Lord from thee.

When I can say my God is mine.  
When I can feel thy glories shine.  
I tread the world beneath my feet.  
And all the earth calls good or great.

Send comforts down from thy right hand.  
While we pass through this barren land.  
And in thy temple let us see.  
A glimpse of love a glimpse of thee.

Hail great Immanuel all divine.  
In thee thy Father's glories shine.  
Thou brightest sweetest fairest one.  
That eyes have seen or angels known.

AS AE AD Jannet Christie 8 of December 1796 Calcutta AP AF AL AR AK

Jannet Christie was probably a pupil at a Mission School in Calcutta. Her sampler uses one coronet and several derivative motifs, and includes a curious collection of initials: AS AE AD AP AF AL AR AK. The hymn is by Dr Isaac Watts, whose first book of *Divine and Moral Songs for Children* had been published in England over seventy-five years earlier.

nor stone, the sweet, soft and delicious strawberry has long been used by artists to symbolize perfect righteousness. Its white flowers often denote innocence and its leaves are almost of the sacred trefoil form.

There was also plenty of religious symbolism in the symmetrically arranged spot motifs of eighteenth-century samplers. For example the peacock is often considered an emblem of Christ in connection with eternal life. Two peacocks flanking a fountain, their feet entangled in vine scrolls, appear frequently in the manuscript pages of early Christian art. As legend had it, peacock flesh did not putrefy, and so the birds became a symbol of the resurrection. They were used in this sense, as a kind of heraldic emblem of Christ, throughout the illuminated manuscripts. From the mid-eighteenth century onwards formal bird patterns, often with the birds in pairs either side of a flower pot, perching on a house or in a tree or drinking at a fountain were one of the most popular sampler motifs in Britain, America and Europe, a clear resemblance to the symbol of eternal life.

The number of crown motifs on eighteenth-century samplers was legion. Sometimes a variety of coronets took up a whole row, but nothing was more useful for filling in a tiny space than a single crown. No doubt the origin of the popularity of this motif is to be found in the fact that linen belonging to a member of the nobility would be marked with the type of coronet that accorded to his or her rank. But many a sampler contains a row of different crown patterns with the following initials either above or below: L  D  Q  GR  P  E  B, standing for Lord, Duke, Queen, George Rex, Prince, Earl, Baron. Generally, this is no more than a decorative pattern in eighteenth-century samplers, although it is possible that a sampler containing just one type of crown indicates that the maker came from noble stock. Occasionally, crowns were turned into a border pattern with alternate ones worked upside-down.

Together with coronets, hearts were also useful for filling in the odd small spaces that an alphabet, for example, might leave at the end of a row. But hearts were not as popular as coronets, and in fact usually appeared only in conjunction with them. There is one tiny, heart-shaped sampler recorded, dated 1796, which is delicately edged with pink frilled ribbon and contains motifs of anchors, hearts, birds, and two pairs of flying cupids. The inscription reads 'be unto me kind and true as I be unto you'. The names Mary Ives, Jane Mumer and Hannah Hopkins were below this, but it is not known which of the three embroidered the piece.

But if the motifs of flowers, birds and crowns were stereotyped and dictated by a teacher, one area where the child could use her own imagination was in representing her own house and family. Increasingly, houses and landscaped scenes conveying vignettes of domestic or rural life were filling up the lower halves of samplers. Elizabeth Cridland's, made in 1752, was fairly typical of those worked in the latter half of the century. She showed her five-windowed house set between two grassy hillocks with a dovecote and small cottage atop one and a windmill on the other. Almost all her animal, flower and bird motifs have exact opposites on either side of the sampler; a tablet at the top of the work contains the Lord's Prayer adorned by four flying cupids. These cupids were commonly seen on eighteenth-century gravestones and were sometimes known as Death's Angels.

Catherine Pickling, aged seven years in 1780, depicted a typical brick Georgian house with two chimneys, a chequered tile entranceway and a tree growing from a vase on either side. Below these are the figures of a man and a woman, probably her parents, as well as two flowers and two hearts. The sampler is extremely well executed for a girl of such tender years.

Parents, when represented on samplers, were rarely identified as such. One of the best-known samplers to contain a portrait of the maker's

Mary Ann Richards' sampler, made in 1800, combines the symmetry of English samplers of the period with an individuality that was more often seen in American examples. An unusual feature is the border within a border at the bottom.

family was worked by another seven-year-old, E. Philips, in 1761. Miss Philips almost crams her sampler with information about her family. In the centre stands a gentleman pointing to his wife and around them stand five girls of various ages, the youngest under the watchful eye of a nurse. In the top right-hand corner a boy is shown with his tutor; opposite them are two maids, one white and one black, reflecting the current fashion as well as the economic standing of the Philips family. There is also a black houseboy shown with a dog. The inclusion of a ship might indicate that Mr Philips was a traveller, perhaps to a land of alligators as one is embroidered alongside the boat.

An utterly charming, late eighteenth-century small sampler,

## Samplers

measuring *c*. 21.9 × 32.5 cm (8¾ × 13 in), is undated and unsigned but includes a portrait of a man with a three-cornered hat and a stick. 'This is my dear father,' the young worker has lovingly embroidered. The man is standing next to a house and the usual complement of birds, trees, animals and cupids worked in simple satin, cross and tent stitch fill up the rest of the woollen canvas.

Many were the odes in gratitude to parents included on eighteenth-century samplers. Among the moral duties of sampler-makers, few were held in such high esteem as that which called for family unity and respect for parental authority. Most of the verses in some way thank parents for providing education, while others thank them for care and guidance in general. It is unlikely, however, that the verse was chosen by the child herself. Two of the most popular were:

Mary Ann Body worked one of the most popular verses of thanks to parents, and surrounded her sampler with a conventional border of strawberries.

> Dear Mother I am young and cannot show
> Such work as I unto your goodness owe
> Be pleased to smile on this my small endeavour
> And I'll strive to learn and be obedient ever.

> Next unto God, dear Parents, I address
> Myself to you in humble Thankfulness
> For all your care on me bestowed
> The means of learning unto me allow'd
> Go on, I pray, and let me still persue
> Those golden Arts the Vulgar never knew.

In 1797 nine-year-old Mary Lewis worked a rather gloomy inscription on the subject of filial duty:

Forget not thy helpless infancy nor the frowardness of thy youth and indulge the infirmities of thy aged parents, assist and support them in the decline of life. So shall their hoary heads go down to the grave in peace, and thine own children in reverence of thy example shall repay thy piety with filial love.

Parents were not the only figures represented. Adam and Eve feature regularly in samplers of the period. There are many variations in the treatment of this subject. In some, Adam and Eve are fully clothed in contemporary costume, in others they are naked but with a generous supply of fig leaves. Occasionally they have clearly been confused with the 'boxer' motif, which had virtually disappeared by the end of the eighteenth century. They often stand by a tree of knowledge, heavily laden with apples. The serpent is a popular decorative motif in its own right, partly because it is the animal which lends itself most easily to interlacing. In connection with Adam and Eve it can be a symbol of evil be-

66

cause it is a memory of the Fall, but it can also be a symbol of eternity and of The Resurrection because it sheds its skin and emerges afresh. A rendering of Adam and Eve would freqently be accompanied by the following jingle:

Adam and Eve whilst innocent
In Paradise were placed
But soon the serpent by his wiles
The happy pair disgraced.

Adam and Eve, the Tree of Knowledge and the Serpent appear below the first four Commandments – 'translated' into rhymes by Dr Isaac Watts in order to help children learn them more easily – in Betty Pleanderleath's 1745 sampler. Mrs Seton was almost certainly Betty's teacher in Edinburgh.

## Samplers

The finely worked silk on linen of this piece resembles the style of the late eighteenth century, though the costume of the shepherdess clearly dates the sampler *c.* 1815. Winged cherubs were popular motifs on eighteenth-century gravestones.

Another verse which no doubt found favour among some early feminists went:

> Adam alone in Paradise did grieve
> And thought Eden a desert without Eve
> Until God, pitying his lonesome state
> Crown'd all his wishes with a lovely mate
> Then why should men think mean or slight her
> That could not live in Paradise without her.

One biblical motif which came into fashion at about this time was the return of the spies Joshua and Caleb from Canaan, carrying a heavy bunch of grapes between them. This motif, however, never acquired great popularity in English samplers and is more often seen in Dutch or American examples.

In addition to these biblical figures, two quite similar samplers at the beginning of the century depicted a richly dressed female holding the orb and sceptre. She is clearly recognizable as Queen Anne, and the initials AR above her head on both occasions identify her beyond doubt. In both she is surrounded by flowers and fruiting trees and it has been suggested that this pattern has its symbolic roots in the enclosed garden of the Holy Virgin in medieval religious art.

Shepherds, shepherdesses and milkmaids are also popular figures, sometimes revealing that the worker has lived on or near a farm. But in the later eighteenth century a shepherdess was usually no more than a figment of the child's imagination and was shown dressed in all the fineries of the day. Ann Day felt that in addition to a crook to watch a single sheep, her shepherdess might need a fan and a hat with three large ostrich feathers. Ann Chapman in 1779 used her very richly dressed and elegantly coiffed shepherd and shepherdess to support a tablet containing Agur's Prayer in which Agur asks two things of the Lord before he dies: to remove vanity and to ensure that he should have neither poverty nor riches – thoughts which do not seem to be shared by the smart couple.

The character of eighteenth-century samplers owed far less to their often rather indifferently worked motifs and patterns than to their sentimental and moralizing verses. Needlework clearly took second place to the instructions for 'upright' living. Many of the verses were concerned with inculcating in young ladies the correct behaviour towards the opposite sex. In particular, verses that appear early in the century are full of this sort of advice. One can almost hear the stern voice of the school mistress ringing through the canvas. Sarah Grimes, working in 1730, must have been a model young lady if she followed her own counsel:

Keep a strict guard over thy tongue, thine ear and thine eye, lest they betray thee to talk things vain and unlawful. Be sparing of thy words, and talk not impertinently or in passion. Keep the parts of thy body in a just decorum, and avoid immoderate laughter and levity of behaviour.

Mary Gardner, aged nine in 1740, quoted from The Proverbs: 'Favour is deceitful, and beauty is vain, But a Woman that feareth the Lord, She shall be praised.' In the same vein, Amy Wilds dated her sampler 31 July 1758 and embroidered that she was taught by Elizabeth Gilbert: 'A silent and loving woman is a gift of the Lord and there is nothing so much worth as a mind well instructed.' Young Elizabeth Bock must have been greatly impressed by the dangers of men after she embroidered the following in 1764:

> Oh Mighty God that knows how inclinations lead
> Keep mine from straying lest my Heart should bleed.
>
> Grant that I honour and succour my parents dear
> Lest I should offend him who can be most severe.
>
> I implore ore me you'd have a watchful eye
> That I may share with you those blessings on high.
>
> And if I should by a young youth be Tempted
> Grant I his schemes defy and all He has invented.

By mid-century most of the inscriptions were in verse form – perhaps doggerel is a more accurate description – and were largely taken from the writings of Dr Isaac Watts, Philip Doddridge and John Wesley. Dr Watts, the son of a non-conformist schoolmaster, helped to set the tone of the majority of samplers in this century with the publication in 1720 of his *Divine and Moral Songs for Children*. He addressed this 'to all that are concerned in the education of children' and explained that 'whatever may conduce to give the minds of children a relish for virtue and religion ... aught to be proposed to you.' Dr Watts believed that what was learned by heart remained longer in the mind, and that his verses would prevent the young from seeking 'relief for an emptiness of mind out of the loose and dangerous sonnets of the age'. Evidently most school mistresses endorsed his views and the ubiquity of his verses on samplers is rivalled only by those of Doddridge and Wesley.

Wesley was a man of deep learning and long-standing Puritan ancestry who passionately wanted to remain a member of the Church of England but, frustrated by what he saw as the Church's apathy, found himself

*Samplers*

a leader of the Methodist movement. The principal object of the movement was the promotion of piety and morality, an intention clearly reflected in samplers. Wesley published twenty-three collections of hymns between 1737 and 1786. Doddridge, a non-conformist theologian, published works of some literary merit as well as writing hymns.

The most popular verses of these men were not religious in the strict sense of the word, but were more concerned with general moral precepts. Fairly typical was one extolling virtue by Isaac Watts:

> Virtue's the chiefest beauty of the mind
> The greatest ornament of human kind
> Virtue's our safeguard and our guiding star
> That stirs up reason when our senses err.

Religious men and women of the day were commonly preoccupied with the imminence of death and the best manner of entering the Heavenly Kingdom. This preoccupation and generally gloomy view of life was also reflected in the samplers and one verse of this kind which, with variations, frequently occurs, is as follows:

> When this you see, remember me,
> And keep me in your mind;
> And be not like the weathercock
> That turn at every wind
> When I am dead and laid in grave,
> And all my bones are rotten,
> By this may I remembered be
> When I should be forgotten.

The samplers of two eight-year-olds show that in spite of their extreme youth they were both already looking forward to the next life. To an extent this is not surprising, as the child mortality rate in the eighteenth century was extremely high. Perhaps the popular verse that Elizabeth Raymond used in 1789 helped many children come to terms with the loss of a sibling or close friend:

> Lord give me wisdom to direct my ways
> I beg not riches nor yet length of days
> My life is a flower, the time it hath to last
> Is mixed with frost and shook with every blast.

Anne Kirk's verse, called 'Live to Die', concluded:

> Let not the Morrow your vain Thoughts employ
> But think this Day the last you shall enjoy.

Anne Kirk's verse seems twice as doom-laden when considering her age. Oval shapes were becoming popular for map samplers at about this time, but were not often used for other kinds of work.

Twelve-year-old Mary Dudden of Cardiff seemed to have a keen appreciation of how to lead a goodly life on Earth. In 1780, beneath an inscription to 'The LIFE of the HAPPY MAN', she embroidered:

The happy Man was born in the city of Regeneration, in the Parish of Repentance unto Life, was educated at the School of Obedience, and now lives in the Plain of Perseverance, he works at the Trade of Diligence, not withstanding he has a large Estate in the County of Christian Contentment and many Times does Jobs of Self-denial.

The following note was attached to the backing board of this sampler: 'Mary Dudden were 12 years of age when this sampler were worked, and some part of it by moonlight.'

The most popular eighteenth-century religious passages were the Ten Commandments, The Lord's Prayer and The Creed, but many other lengthy extracts from the Bible were often embroidered on samplers. These would usually be set out within tablets similar to those painted and hung in contemporary churches. They were often flanked by biblical figures such as Moses or Jesus. Jane Brumfit of Leeds chose Aaron, Moses and Joshua to surround her tablets of the Ten Commandments. Ann Divitt was nine when she worked a beautiful sampler in 1722 with the story of Jacob and his brothers, first in words and then pictorially. Three winged cherubs cast a watchful eye over two panels with an impressive crown between them. Such an amount of lettering was quite a feat but it was not at all unknown for whole chapters of the Bible to be embroidered and the long 134th Psalm was a favourite among sampler workers. A rhyming version of the Ten Commandments by Isaac Watts was deemed useful by many teachers as an *aide-memoire*. Occasionally, Welsh language samplers were made which were usually plain sombre pieces comprising only verses and alphabets and little ornament. They would doubtless have been made at home as the Welsh language and culture were forbidden in schools at that time. These pieces clearly reflect the strict discipline and uprightness of the Methodist environment from which they sprang.

Towards the latter part of the century some new kinds of samplers were being made. In many cases these were merely departures further into the realms of school exercises and suggest only that one school teacher was vying with another to find the most original guise for so-called samplers. From about 1770 onwards map samplers were popular. Some of these covered just a small district or county; others shared two hemispheres, one marked The Old World, the other The New World. Maps of single countries including France, Spain and Ireland were also made. One characteristic of most map samplers was inaccuracy, partly because

Elizabeth Hawkins included many of the geographical conventions often found on map samplers; 'German Ocean' was almost always used for the North Sea. Dark green silk has been used to make the sea appear dark and the countries are outlined in rows of cross stitch.

OPPOSITE Arnolds Farm, Essex, worked in coloured silk on wool.

names were often embroidered wherever there was a space, not always where they belonged, and partly because the outlines were often drawn freehand by the children. For example, Anne Brown, aged eleven, thought the coasts of France and England were somehow joined. School-mistresses were, no doubt, responsible for some of the more exact outlines, and it was also possible to buy map outlines commercially printed, usually on satin. The name of the publisher would often be embossed at the bottom.

One of the most lovingly executed pieces of local history is an unsigned, undated 'Map of the Farm called Arnolds in the parishes of Stapleford Abby and Lambourn in the County of Essex being part of the estate of . . .' There is room left in the cartouche for the owner's name but unfortunately it was never included, although the names of neighbouring landowners, including the Earl of Granville, have been listed. Some portraits of striking local birds have been added, as well as domestic pets and a small barn at the top, near a river.

A far more common type of map was that showing England and Wales with 'part of Scotland and part of Ireland'. A popular method of making the counties stand out was to outline them with three rows of chenille thread, while the lettering was usually worked in cross or Algerian eye stitch. A wreath or scroll, usually placed in the North Sea,

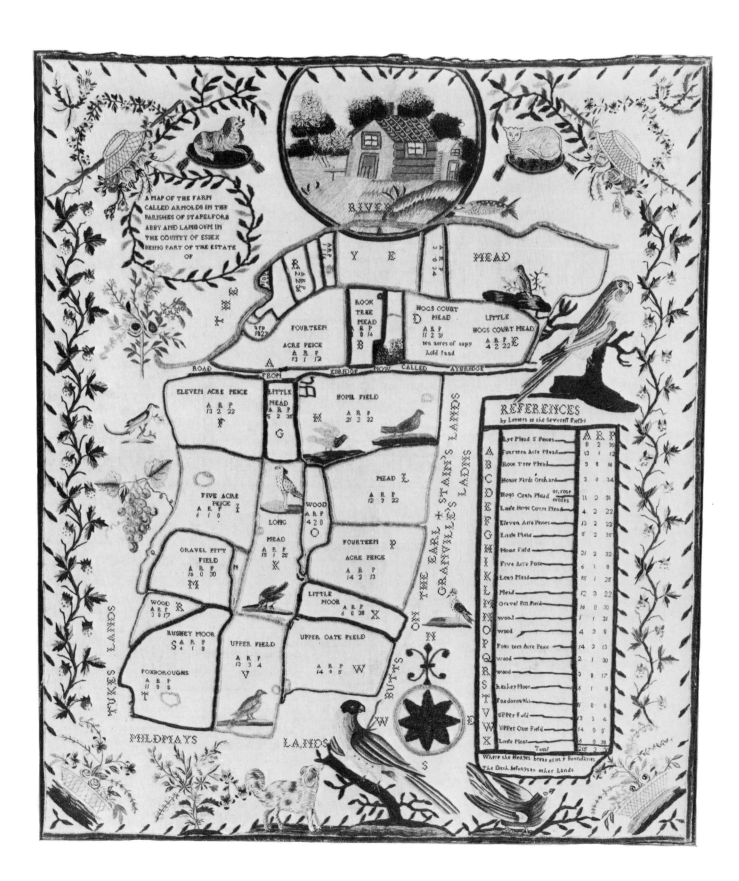

## Samplers

RIGHT Elizabeth Brassey, a pupil at Mrs Tapley's School in Chester, executed an extremely detailed county map of England and Wales, noting towns and areas of importance. Today Dunmow, in Essex, is little more than a village; Brightelmstone has become Brighton. Sadly, the colours on this sampler have run in the years since it was made.

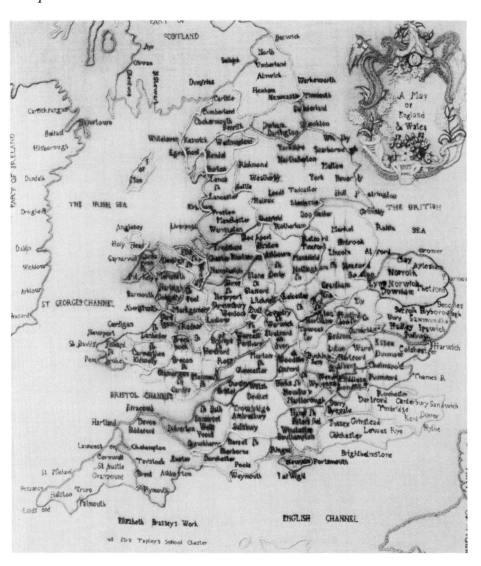

OPPOSITE ABOVE Elizabeth Knowles included complex instructions for using the almanac she worked in 1787: 'Under the Word Years find the Year above which is the Dominical letter for that Year, then against the Month in the other Table find the same letter over which are placed the Days of the Month for every Sunday of that Month.'

OPPOSITE MIDDLE Rebus sampler worked in 1793 by Elizabeth Bullock.

OPPOSITE BELOW Memorial acrostic sampler by T.B.

would contain the worker's name and date of completion and often the school where it was worked. Sometimes Britannia ruling the waves was also included. Many of these maps were oval, a shape not usually seen in other samplers, and most were sewn either on linen or fine gauze. Many contained a variety of ships on the high seas while others were lent a touch of reality by having dark green silk under the fine material in order to make the pale-coloured land stand out more clearly.

Almost all maps contained points of the compass, but a scale of miles, or lines of longitude and latitude, were less common. Far more often a flowing garland of flowers and bows would be used to surround the map. An unusual oval map of Africa, made in 1784 at Mrs Arnold's

74

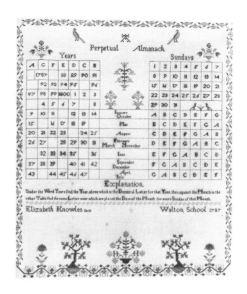

## The Schoolroom Products

Fetherston Buildings, is surrounded with such a border of embroidered flowers and bows, embellished with spangles, the eighteenth-century term for sequins. The map is full of place names, some now obsolete but none the less evocative: Grain coast, Tooth coast, Slave coast.

At about the same time that maps were popular, other school exercise samplers included almanacs, acrostic, rebus and darning samplers. Two almost identical almanac samplers are known to have been made at Walton school. One is signed 'Ellen Stackhouse fecit 1781' and the other 'Elizabeth Knowles fecit 1787'. Both name the school. The two vary only slightly in shape and in the ornament below the almanac. They are made in silk on cotton in cross and Algerian eye stitches. This 'Perpetual Almanack' with instructions for its use, was obviously the invention of a teacher. Perhaps it was given only to the star pupils of the needlework class as both are exemplary pieces.

Rebus samplers, or those where pictures are used instead of words, are not often seen. Elizabeth Bullock, aged ten in 1793, worked one with the inscription: 'Noah sent forth a [dove] out of the [ark] that came to him again in the evening with an olive [leaf] that she had plucked and brought in her [beak]. So Noah knew that the waters were abated from off the earth.' The words in brackets were replaced by pictures.

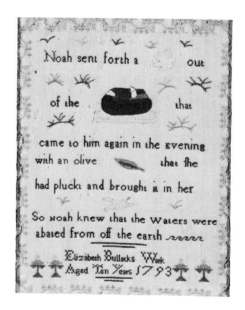

Acrostic samplers, in which the first letters of a line spell a word vertically, were far more popular at this time. Favourite names to be worked in this way included Christ and the embroiderer's close relatives. The following verse was worked by 'T.B':

An Acrostic
On My Late Dear Sister
Jane Emery Day
died Sepr 14 1792

Jealous of Self. deeply possess'd
And rested twas within her breast
No allowed sin in her was seen
Early forsook bane paths of sin.

Earnestly She enquired th'way to God
Marked well She did. each step She trod
Eager pursued it through CHRIST's Blood
Righteousness divind She gloried in
Yea Confessed herself nought in sin.

Dearly highly favoured Youth thou
Ascended art to JESUS now
Yields Him the Crown eternal through.

## Samplers

It was quite common for samplers to refer in passing to the ruling king, but commemorative samplers containing glowing references to departed monarchs were rare. Elizabeth Dick, aged ten, embroidered the following in 1726, towards the end of George I's reign:

> God bless King George
> Preserve the Crown
> Defend the Church
> Cast rebells down.

In 1782 Elizabeth Spencer worked a longer, more stirring piece of patriotism entitled 'On King George':

> Long may the King Great Britain's Sceptre Sway While all his
> Subjects peacably obey. And when God's Providence shall him remove
> From these below to highest Realms above. To his own Race may
> he the Crown resign For ever to continue in that Line.

Two kinds of eighteenth-century sampler stand out above the rest as containing some very fine and elaborate examples of needlework, as well as being closer approximations of the original pattern record sampler. These are the darning and hollie point samplers.

The simple darning samplers were no doubt the work of school-children and were designed to respond to the necessity of darning the flimsy muslin dresses and damask tablecloths of the day. The darns were worked in two different colours by the counted thread method, usually in the shape of a cross. This made a most attractive pattern where the two shades met and also had the advantage of enabling a teacher quickly to spot a mistake. Many of the darns were in fact worked over specially cut holes or L-shaped tears. These schoolroom darning pieces were often signed and dated. E. Cousens chose an original way to do this; in the centre of twelve darns she worked:

E Cousens

march the     27      finished this
              1777

Darning peice

Many other darning pieces were unsigned and undated and contained elaborate floral patterns worked in pattern darning with stem and chain stitches used to outline the leaves and flowers. Usually these bouquets

LEFT A darning sampler from the Netherlands worked by A V, aged 14, in 1777.

ABOVE Darning samplers probably originated in Germany, but they soon became an important part of the basic needlework training in English schools. This sampler was worked in the last quarter of the 18th century. The pattern darning in the middle could often turn otherwise strictly practical pieces into highly decorative works.

were placed in the middle of the darns and a border of simple drawn threadwork would complete the piece. These samplers are generally thought to have been worked by adult needlewomen, as few children executed proficiency on this level in other samplers of the day.

One other kind which displayed a high degree of technical ability was the often rather small, linen thread on linen sampler of designs in hollie or holy point, sometimes called nun's work. The name derived from the point lace stitch used in church work by medieval religious houses and is similar to the technique of needlepoint lace. Unfinished samplers have been found which indicate the method of working. First, circles or bands were cut out of the fabric and edged with buttonholing. Then rows of buttonholing were built up, one into another. The pattern was made by missing stitches, which appear as fine pin pricks on an even white ground. The designs were very simple and included formal geometric (often diamond) patterns, hearts, crowns, acorns, flowers and stars. Sometimes initials, dates, and mottoes such as 'sweet baby' were

worked. Hollie point samplers usually included small panels of cutwork and were sometimes bordered with rows of whitework.

These samplers have much in common with those of an earlier century, not only because of the quality of workmanship but because they were of practical value. Hollie point was most useful for ventilated insertions and open seams on baby clothes; it also looked very dainty. Two eighteenth-century hollie point samplers are interesting in that they are not the conventional square shape and were clearly intended to serve as a useful pattern reference for clothes-making. In 1741 Amy Malsey worked a piece of linen with eight elongated 'U' shapes and one oval filled with hollie point insertions. Fifty years later, Ann Blake made a very similar piece with two of the filled 'U' shapes and one slim panel containing her name and the date, 1791. Both would have served admirably as guides for making delicate seam insertions on small shirts.

The general quality of eighteenth-century samplers leaves little doubt that moral and religious instruction was often more important than the needlework. Sewing itself is rarely a subject for homilies but Mary Miller in 1735 worked the following:

> No surplice white the priest could wear
> Bandless the bishop must appear
> The King without a shirt would be
> Did not the needle help all three.

But the tone of Mary Cole's verse in 1759 was a much more accurate reflection of contemporary values:

> Better by far for Me
> than all the Simpster's Art
> That God's commandments be
> Embroider'd on my Heart.

# 4
# America's Blossoming Tradition

The story of the eighteenth-century American colonists is a curious blend of extreme hardship and struggle with growing affluence and prosperity. In the first half of the century the daily life of colonial women was one of unremitting toil; building up their new country involved sharing the toughest tasks with husbands and sons in addition to taking care of many of the traditional womanly duties. There were forests to be cleared, fields to be cultivated, candles, soaps and baskets to be made as well as child-rearing, cooking, spinning, weaving, dyeing and knitting. Above all, basic plain sewing played a vital part in every woman's life. Ready-made fabrics were far too expensive for most of the colonists, which meant that the women had to start from scratch in making clothing for their family. Since it might take as long as a year and a half to turn flax into linen, this was a time-consuming project. And it was not only clothes that were required; sheets, towels, warm bedcoverings, rugs and other household goods were also essential, and were usually the only means by which many of these early settlers could adorn their homes. Yet in spite of the sheer volume of all they had to do, most colonial women took great pride in their needlework.

The wars against the French and Indians in the 1740s and '50s took their toll in lives and land, and brought much destruction and devastation to the early settlements that had so painfully been built up. But at the same time many colonists took advantage of the wars to make their fortunes, for although America was a Puritan-dominated society, accumulating wealth was certainly not considered a sin. Rather, it was a sure sign of Heaven-willed success. And so, at about the same time as a prosperous middle class was securing its stake in England, its American counterpart was growing both in size and material prosperity. Between 1700

OPPOSITE Lucy Stickney's graceful sampler is worked in silk and paint on linen. The reflection of the house in the water is an unusual decorative feature for a sampler, and she may have specifically chosen the verse to go with the scene.

*Samplers*

and 1770 the population of the American colonies jumped from 629,000 to 2,148,000 and by 1800 it had reached 5,000,000. This growth was concentrated in Boston, Newport, New York, Philadelphia, and Charleston, which were, by the end of the century, no longer outposts of a wilderness but major seaports.

The middle classes of these small cities were sufficiently rich and sophisticated to require houses grand enough to display their taste in the visual arts; they also enjoyed watching plays, listening to music and reading.

At first, the cultural appetites of the successful American colonists were satisfied by imports from the mother country. This was as true in the field of domestic, decorative arts where a piece brought over from England was considered especially notable, as it was in the field of literature. But a change followed the Seven Years' War. The British Parliament was then reluctantly forced to concern itself more actively with the thirteen American colonies and, in particular, with financing the defence of colonial frontiers so as to relieve the British taxpayer. The series of revenue-raising solutions proposed by the mother country caused increasing resistance and riot in America. By 1773 the Royal Governor of Massachusetts, Thomas Hutchinson, had declared that 'no line can be drawn between the supreme Authority of Parliament and the total Independence of the colonies', to which the radical organizations such as the Sons of Liberty responded that 'If there can be no such line, the consequence is either that the Colonies are the vassals of Parliament, or that they are totally Independent. As it cannot be supposed that we should be reduced to a state of Vassalage, the conclusion is ... that we were thus Independent ...' This hardening of attitude and the Americans' sense of their own worth was soon to be reflected in the growth of a native art and culture. As in England, the vital complement to the growth of the middle classes had been the education of children and, as far as the girls were concerned, this had meant a grounding not only in the basic skills of literacy and numeracy but also in music, dancing, painting and needlework of the practical and ornamental kind, generally referred to as plain and fancy work.

There was always mending and marking to be done – linens that had taken so long to make were a very precious commodity – as well as making the decorative pieces which indicated the family's social standing. Tambour- and crewelwork were the most popular techniques for these. No girl could be considered marriageable without mastery of needlework. In any event, it was considered alluring to the opposite sex for a young woman to be sitting with a piece of embroidery in her hands,

Laura Hyde's sampler of 1800 combines commentary and pictorial references to far-off India with the more conventionally American motif of the Eagle. The exotic scenes are unusual, but were probably inspired by a teacher; a very similar sampler made in the same part of Connecticut depicts the Levant. Here the wife of the British Ambassador is seen on a visit to a local harem.

and the framed sampler, usually given pride of place in the front parlour or sitting room, was, for all suitors to see, a certificate of her ability.

A sampler was the starting point in American educational establishments for all needlework forms whether plain or fancy. Both kinds were taught in schools and whether a child learned one kind or the other, or both, was largely determined by her family's financial status. Although the sampler was generally considered plain sewing, often young girls would make two kinds. The first, for marking purposes, would chiefly comprise alphabets and numerals and might even be taught by a mother at home. The second would contain pictorial elements and would display some effort at design; it would be made under instruction in a fashionable Ladies' Academy or Seminary, and later framed. The latter have survived in greater numbers partly because they were always intended to be preserved.

From around 1750 samplers had taken on a distinctive American flavour, revealing less of the formality, discipline and symmetry of English examples and more spirited individuality and unrestrained liveliness. And after about 1800 samplers, like other art forms, were also imbued with the spirit of republicanism, and featured symbols of Liberty, the American Eagle and other patriotic themes. Although women were afforded better educations after the War of Independence, American society still placed much the same value on needlework for

*Samplers*

girls as did the contemporary English world, and so the sampler continued to thrive.

American samplers, while rich in inventiveness and spirit, none the less reflected a debt to the sixteenth-century European pattern books. The samplers made before 1700 differed hardly at all from their English counterparts, and although few were made between 1700 and 1750 those that survive show that they were still made in the cross-band form with motifs clearly derivative of those in English and continental samplers. From mid-century, when the imported fashion was turned into a uniquely American art form, the designs still contained certain fixed elements – an alphabet, numerals, a verse, the maker's name and the date of the work, several small scenes and, as a focal point, a wide border. But even within this formula there was enormous scope for freshness and variety.

The originality of American samplers depended for a large part on the talents of the schoolmistress, one or two of whom have received posthumous fame through the samplers of their charges. These teachers were constantly advertising their skills at various types of hand work including waxwork, quillwork, shellwork, japanning, tambour work and crewelwork, as well as proclaiming their ability to watch over the morals and manners of their potential pupils. A large number were from England, a fact about which they boasted in their announcements in American newspapers. Mary Gray used the *New-York Mercury* of 8 October 1753 for the following notice:

Plain Work. Lately arrived in this city from Great Britain, Mrs Mary Gray who professes teaching all sorts of Plain work in the neatest manner, Dresden work in all its varieties; Ladies capuchine and Children's frocks in the newest fashion, Ladies that have a desire of seeing any of her work may see it at Captain Heysham's, in the upper end of Broad Street near the City Hall where the said Mrs Gray teaches. Likewise teaches to work ladies Gloves.

On 20 May 1765, the same newspaper carried a similar advertisement for Mary Bosworth:

Mary Bosworth, Lately from London, takes this method to inform the public, that she has opened a school in Cortlandt street, near Mr John Lary's; wherein she teaches young masters and misses to read and learn them all sorts of verse; she likewise learns young ladies plain work, samplairs, Dresden flowering on cat gut, shading with silk or worsted, on Cambrick, lawn or Holland; she draws all sorts of lace in the genteelest manner. Those gentlemen and ladies that will be pleased to favour her with care of their children, may be assured that she will make them her chief study to deserve their approbation.

OPPOSITE This eighteenth-century Spanish sampler carries beautiful and intricate designs worked in satin, double-running and overcast back stitches with bullion knots, on linen.

84

Sophia Ellis
finished this Work
february the 8 1785 In
the 9 year of her age

## America's Blossoming Tradition

Many of the women pointed out that certain other types of fancy work could also be taught at extra cost.

There were hundreds of teachers, not all of them women, who set up school during the second half of the century; some of them survived just a few short terms, others taught for several years. Successful establishments had to move quite frequently into bigger and better premises. The best of the pictorial sampler work was done by girls aged twelve to sixteen at the female seminaries or academies, the select schools which took in both boarding and day girls. The earliest and the finest were along the eastern seaboard, especially in the Boston area.

The diary of Anna Green Winslow, written in 1771, contains a record of one Boston school. One year previously Anna, then aged ten, had been sent far away from her home in Nova Scotia to Boston, the birthplace of her parents, where she was to be 'finished' at a Boston school. From her diary we learn that she was very industrious and full of domestic accomplishments as well as conscientious about her religion. She could make fine network, knit lace, and spin linen thread and woollen yarn. She could make purses and embroider pocket books, weave watchstrings and piece patchwork. Even when she had painful whitloes on her finger she wrote: 'It will be a nice opportunity ... to perfect myself in learning to spin flax.' On 9 March she wrote:

A very snowy day. I have been a very good girl today about my work however ... in the first place I sew'd on the bosom of unkle's shirt, mended two pair of gloves, mended for the wash two handkerchiefs (one cambrick), sewed on half a border of a lawn apron of aunts, read part of the XXIst chapter of Exodus and a story in the Mother's gift.

Small wonder, if that was a typical day, that Anna and her generation needed to know how to sew!

Teachers were not the only commodity 'newly arrived' from London. A Mrs Condy, who was living near the Old North Meeting House in Boston, announced in the *Boston News-Letter* of 4 May 1738 that she was selling 'all sorts of beautiful Figures on Canvas for Tent Stick [stitch]'. She explained that although the patterns originated from London, she could produce a much less expensive version by drawing them on the canvas herself. She also advertised 'all sorts of Canvas, without drawing'. It may be assumed that the drawings were for all sorts of embroidery.

Generally, however, all linen was homespun, necessitated largely by the heavy tax on imports, and much of that used for samplers was unbleached, of an open weave and rather coarse. Sometimes it was coloured either tan, light brown or bottle green or, very occasionally,

OPPOSITE A vibrant, well designed example worked in 1785 by Sophia Ellis gracefully combines religious and secular motifs.

grey or black. Tammy, or woollen, grounds were used far less than in England at this time and tiffany would not become popular until the early nineteenth century. A recent study has found that some American samplers between 1798 and 1832 were embroidered on linsey–woolsey, a mixture of wool and flax, although no English examples on this material are known.

As in England, silk was the most popular embroidery thread for samplers, with some linen used and, very occasionally, wool. Silk yarns and fabrics became much more accessible after the revolutionary war when America began trading directly with China. Some of the silk used had a crinkled appearance, as if it had been unwound from tightly twisted hanks, and this gave the work an unusual, shimmering effect.

Almost all the thread used in the eighteenth century was home-dyed. Some dyestuffs were imported but these were extremely costly, and so the choice of colours and shades was fairly limited for colonial women. They searched constantly for new sources of natural dyes and better ways of ensuring that they stayed fast. Cochineal and indigo were the most expensive of the imported dyes but, even so, it was quite usual for houses to have an indigo-tub in the rear kitchen. Other popular dyes were made from onions for yellows, black walnut bark for browns and elderberries for a lavender colour. Some shades of brown were made from rust, which has subsequently eaten away background material wherever it was used. Even if the number of colours was restricted, American samplers stand out for the imaginative use made of the thread.

Those worked at Miss Sarah Stivour's school in Salem, Massachusetts, are all notable for a very long stitch in crinkled or ravelled silk. This stitch, placed diagonally in parallel lines, gave a rich look and texture to the background of pieces where it was used. At least 5 cm (2 in) long and sometimes more, the stitches in green at the bottom represented grass; those in blue and white overhead indicated the sky. Samplers with this kind of stitch, sometimes called Stivour stitch, were generally all arranged in a similar fashion with a landscape at the bottom, perhaps including a man and a woman, some sheep which might be stuffed, and a dog. Around them on three sides and possibly worked into the sky would be a floral border of large blooms emanating from two trees. Winged cherubs often surveyed the scene. The border with the landscape incorporated was the focal point, and confined to a small square in the centre were alphabets and a verse, probably containing the maker's name and the date – all that remained of the conventional English type.

Two of the earliest examples, worked by Stivour pupils Nabby Mason Peele and Ruthey Putnam, were both dated 1778, and both named the

Dorothy Ashton's 1764 sampler employs the distinctive silk stitching that was favoured by the Stivour school, yet she worked her piece long before the years in which the school is thought to have been in existence (*c.* 1778–86). The birds, stag, tree, leopard, shepherd and shepherdess are all outlined in fine black thread and the shepherd has small sequins on his costume as an added embellishment.

school. In ten-year-old Ruthey's piece it is possible to see the original ink sketch lines below the silk. The samplers are interesting because they show the early use at the school of the long, kinky silk stitches when the skyline was indicated in an extremely modern, impressionistic manner by just a few strokes of different colours at opposing angles. In a 1784 sampler by Sally Bott and another by Mary Richardson in 1783, the whole border areas were filled in with the diagonal ravelled silk threads behind people, flowers, birds and trees; it is thought that these two were also made at the school.

It is not safe to attribute all samplers which make use of this distinctive silk to the Sarah Stivour school, although it is likely that such pieces were made in the Salem area. Salem was a port of some significance at the time and it is thought that American sea captains brought back this type of silk from China and Japan. In 1764, thirteen-year-old Dorothy Ashton made a sampler with real depth to it by using the kinky silk to cover her entire background area. But her stitches were placed mostly vertically, not diagonally. She couched down the long stitches used on her leopard to give an effect of black spots, and added metal threads and sequins to embellish a seated shepherd. The piece was almost certainly made in or around Salem although Dorothy does not name her school. The sampler shares some characteristics with Sally Bott's piece, but it was made fourteen years before the Stivour school is known to have been in existence.

Samplers made at the school run by Miss Mary (Polly) Balch in Providence, Rhode Island, are perhaps the best known and most sophisticated of any single group of American samplers. It is quite likely that only the best of those made at the Academy between 1785 and 1799 have survived as evident Balch-school products while others made there by girls of lesser ability, who were consequently given much simpler designs, go unrecognized. The samplers of Miss Balch's school, which took boarding and day pupils and was one of the finest of its day, combined detailed architectural motifs with landscape, figures and occasionally a maritime scene, thus achieving some of the most elaborate effects ever seen on American examples. Many are inscribed Providence, but none specifically names the Balch Academy. Much research has gone into identifying samplers with definite links to the school. The manner in which the entire background of the piece is usually filled with diagonal pattern darning is one of the major distinguishing features. This gives the finished work a tapestry-like effect and must have demanded much patience from the pupils. The central portion is, in most of the examples, a major public building, university or church flanked by elegant pillars or arches. These are often worked in simple stitches but through clever use of colour and perspective they appear three-dimensional. They would be framed by a graceful floral border on two or three sides, almost always growing out of pots or urns. Occasionally, a triple border is used as in Eunice Lincoln's large sampler which features a house and figures surrounded by two columns, then a floral border, then a geometric border and finally a thin diamond-patterned border.

Two of the most popular buildings represented in Balch-school samplers were the Old State House in Providence and the Old University Hall at Brown University. In 1786 Nabby Martin embroidered both, as well as a number of figures and decorative motifs, below an inscription that read:

> to Colleges and Schools ye YouthS repair
> Improve each preciouS Moment while you're there.

She gave the University Hall one less storey than the four it should have had. Nancy Hall and Sally Alger included interpretations of the first

Polly Spurr's lovely, and accurate, embroidery of the façade of the First Congregational Church in Providence. From the Balch Academy, 1796.

President's reception at the College in their pictures of the University Hall. In 1794, Susan Smith made one of the most ambitious of the Balch-school samplers when she portrayed the First Baptist Meeting House in Providence. Amazingly, it apparently took her just six months to complete as the date 29 October 1793 appears in the top half with 'wrought this May 9 1794' at the bottom. Polly Spurr was eleven when she made a beautifully vivid sampler featuring the First Congregational Church in Providence, omitting none of the intricate architectural details of this imposing structure. The Balch family is known to have worshipped at the wooden church, which was built in 1795, one year before Polly Spurr's sampler. The church was destroyed by fire on 14 June 1814.

But Balch-school samplers were not restricted to buildings. Eliza Cozzens in 1795 and Hannah Carlile in 1796 made a copious basket of fruit the subject of their pieces. Eliza enclosed hers within the familiar columns surrounded by a floral border while Hannah added a small landscape and a memorial verse:

> Lilies blended with the Rose Now no more adorn her face
> Nor her Cheek with Blushes glow Adding Charms to ev'ry grace.

Hannah's mother, Phebe Aborn Carlile, had died in 1785.

## Samplers

'Let virtue be a guide to thee' was the maxim most frequently worked on Balch school samplers. This example is by Cynthia Burr, aged 15, 1786. Worked in multicoloured silks, it shows the State House in the middle and University Hall in the top border.

Nancy Winsor was one of a very few American school girls to make a seascape the centre of her sampler. Within a twisted pole-style arch she embroidered a large sailing ship and a small raft with several people examining the big vessel through telescopes. A bouquet of flowers tied with a large bowknot sets off the whole scene, and there is even room for a small landscape at the bottom. The piece is dated 4 December 1786. It is quite possible that Nancy went on to make a second elaborate sampler as there is a record of Olney Winsor, thought to have been her father, writing to his wife in 1787 and saying that he had written to Miss Balch about finding a design for his daughter's sampler. Olney Winsor was working in Alexandria, Virginia, at the time and had had to tell Miss Balch that he could not send a draft of a suitable building. Instead, he suggested that the State House be the centrepiece of his daughter's work 'for it is the best proportioned building I have seen'. He continued: 'I hope Nancy is not kept so close to working on her sampler as to injure her eyes, or her health by too steady sitting – you justly observe that is a great piece of work for such a child – therefore great care should be taken to give her proper times of relaxation.'

A few of the Balch samplers contained short verses, but most included just one or two aphorisms such as 'Honour and renown will the ingenious crown', or 'May spotless innocence and truth my every action guide and guard my unexperienced youth from arrogance and pride'. The favourite Balch Academy maxim was 'Let virtue be a guide to thee', on occasions embellished with the following words: 'Virtue outshines the stars, outlives the tombs, climbs up to heaven and finds a peaceful home.' Maxims about virtue had a long history in English samplers but the word acquired a rather special meaning for Americans after the War of Independence. They argued that virtue was the cement of liberty and that it was therefore essential for a population to remain virtuous if it was to retain a free government. And so virtue passed into the patriotic and revolutionary vocabulary, implying qualities such as honesty and prudence, forbearance and piety.

A sampler by Polly Turner worked in 1786 tells us much about the methods used at the Balch school. Her embroidery was done through paper, which is visible on the back. The paper, taken from a newspaper of 19 May, 1786, was used only under the areas that were embroidered. It is also possible to see the ink drawing on the cloth which served as an outline under the floral trails of the outside border. Although the sampler is badly stained and in fragile condition, it can be seen that the composition was an ambitious one. Eight people have been embroidered, the ladies dressed in fashionably striped skirts with metallic threads used sparingly, but effectively to adorn their costumes. The rest of the work, in silk thread on a linen ground, comprised cross, stem, satin and rococo stitches – the usual Balch repertoire. Rococo-stitched floral borders, recognizable from the evenly spaced holes that the pattern leaves, were a particular favourite.

The identity of the needlework teacher at the school has never been exactly determined. Whoever she was can take credit for a large amount of imaginative and vigorous work, though she was not prepared to see bold designs compromise the highest standards. It is quite possible that the mother of Polly Balch, Sarah Rogers Balch, was the guiding force of the needlework rooms because the originality of design diminished after 1811, the year in which she died. Although the school is referred to as Miss Mary Balch's Academy, it is quite clear that it was a family enterprise. It is highly improbable that Mary Balch herself was the teacher; a surviving family register sampler worked by her shows none of the sparks of imagination displayed by her pupils. She died on 5 January 1831. Many samplers that bear a close resemblance to those known to have been worked at the Balch Academy were probably made under the supervision of young teachers who had themselves attended Miss Balch's school.

A third distinctive group of samplers comprised those made at schools in Pennsylvania. These often name the teacher concerned, the most famous being Mrs Leah Meguier, who taught at Harrisburg. Mrs Meguier has been identified as the wife of one Isaac Maguire, a tavern-keeper and bootmaker. The borders of the samplers worked in her school were divided into some eighteen or twenty-two, 2.5-cm (1-in) squares, each containing motifs such as hearts, flowers, birds, a basket of eggs, geometric shapes or butterflies. An inscription would usually take up the bottom two or three squares. For example, Barbara A. Baner worked the following text below a panel containing her name, her parents' names, her birthplace and date, the name of the school and the date she made the sampler:

> And must this body die this mortal frame
> decay and must those active limbs of
> mine lie mouldring in the clay. And there
> for to remain until Christ doth please to come.

The squared border in these pieces acted as a frame for a small inner border of a more conventional floral nature. Within this, the central section featured a woman, sometimes alone with a wreath of roses on one arm and carrying a garland of roses, and sometimes sharing the square with a couple. A weeping willow was a common motif of these pictures.

Betsy Davis's 1797 sampler is another fine example of the Balch tradition, worked in silk on linen. The flowers have been executed in rococo stitch.

Ann E. Kelley in 1826 made the face of the woman in her sampler by
painting it on paper first and then pasting it to the underside of her sheer
fabric, in this case an open mesh cotton. Painted faces, sometimes pasted
or painted directly on to the background, were an innovation that was
especially popular in the early nineteenth century. In addition to saving
time, this method also helped to create a more realistic effect.

Other teachers in the area who produced similarly elaborate work included Mrs Leah Galligher in Lancaster and Mrs Welchan in Maytown.
Samplers at their schools were generally worked on a fine linen or muslin
gauze, which meant that the threads on the underside connecting one word
to the next clearly showed through. These samplers would often be
bound in a variety of ways including gold braid and white satin demask.

Another type of ribbon border also associated with samplers worked
in Pennsylvania and occasionally New Jersey, used pleated or quilled
silk ribbon, often with ornate rosettes in the four corners. Mary Ann
Stauffer of East Hempfield bound her piece with flat green silk, which
she then decorated with two rows of pink silk ribbon, quilled and inter-
twined.

Literally hundreds of sampler-makers inscribed the following:

> This work of mine my friends may have
> When I am dead and in my grave
> This I did to let you see
> What care my parents took of me.

Barbara A Baner a Daughter of Joseph
and Esther Baner was Born in york M
arch the 20 in the year of our Lord 1793
and made this Sampler in Harrisburgh in
Mrs Leah Meguier School A D 1812
And must this body die this mortal frame
decay and must those active limbs of
mine lie mouldring in the clay And there
for to remain until Christ doth please to
come

ABCDEFGHIKL
MNOPQRSTUV
WXYZ ABCDEF
GHIJKLMNOPQ
RSTUVWWXYZ
ABCDEFGHIIKLMNOPQRST
UVWXYZ abcdefghijklmnopqr
stuvwxyz&

The rising morning can't assure
That we shall end the day!
For death stands ready at the door,
To take our lives away.
Ann E England
1820

But Pennsylvania girls often specified that their work was a present for their parents, in words similar to those used by Elizabeth Miskey in 1822. She said: 'Respectfully presented to Anthony and Elizabeth Miskey by their affectionate daughter Elizabeth Miskey done in her 12th year, Philadelphia April 26th 1822.'

Samplers made in Pennsylvania by those of German or Dutch descent are distinctive products more akin to the European tradition of samplers than any other kind made in America. They contain no charming landscaped scenes, nor even verses or alphabets, but a series of rather angular motifs scattered around the sampler in a more or less orderly fashion. The most common motifs were six-pointed stars, square-topped hearts, coronets, straight flower stems growing out of vases and the much-loved, long-tailed peacocks, usually in pairs facing each other. Since most of the embroidery was executed in cross stitch it was difficult to make curves or filled-in flowers. Even the lettering was straight-edged and stiff.

OPPOSITE Ann E. England's beautiful, well composed sampler is one of three pieces made between 1816–35 which bear remarkably similar characteristics and were probably designed by the same teacher.

LEFT Susana Landis, working in 1826, filled her sampler with classic motifs such as peacocks, stags, hearts, coronets and a proliferation of initials. Her piece is more similar to German samplers of the time than to contemporary American ones.

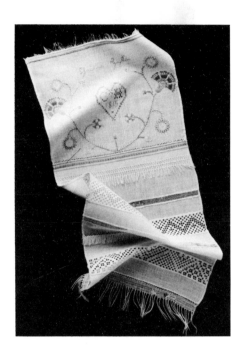

A cotton miniature show towel made by Christina Hessin in 1815.

## Samplers

These pieces rarely had a border, other than perhaps a silk ribbon binding, and they come closer to the original purpose of samplers than most other types. They were made as patterns for the delicate hand towels and other articles of household linen the girls would be expected to embroider. The hand towels, sometimes called show towels or even sampler towels, were usually embroidered in red and blue thread and displayed names, alphabets, and some drawn threadwork as well as a variety of cross-stitched motifs. Made from the 1780s to the 1880s, they often had two small loops sewn to the top indicating that they were intended to be used, but it is doubtful if many of them dried more than a few pairs of hands.

A small group of German settlers in Pennsylvania was responsible for founding one of the finest early American boarding schools. The group, which had emigrated to Pennsylvania in 1741, pursued the Protestant doctrines of the Reformation martyr John Huss and, under the auspices of the Moravian Church or Church of the United Brethren, had established by 1749 a boarding school in Bethlehem, Pennsylvania. This progressive girls' school soon acquired a high reputation and in 1785 it was decided to allow girls of other faiths to attend. It then became known as the Moravian female seminary and was patronized by some of the country's finest families. But even at a school like this, which offered a relatively radical curriculum in terms of academic instruction for girls, a wide range of needlework skills including knitting and sampler-making was still considered an important aspect of every young lady's schooling. The mind was not to be cultivated at the expense of the hands.

Also in Pennsylvania, the Quakers or Society of Friends were making a distinctive contribution both to girls' education in general and to American sampler traditions in particular. The best known of these Quaker schools was the Westtown school, Chester County, which opened in 1799 and is still in operation. There was another big Friends' school in Dutchess County, New York, known as the Nine Partners Boarding School.

The Westtown School was described in the State Annals of Pennsylvania in 1843 as being 'among the most distinguished of the seminaries of learning in the country' and was 'to furnish, besides the requisite portion of literary instruction, an education exempt from the contagion of vicious example and calculated to establish habits and principles favourable to future usefulness in religious and civil society'. With these goals in mind, it is hardly surprising that Quaker school samplers are much less elaborate than other types. The earliest consist of a simple oval border of vines and leaves around a few geometric motifs and a characteristic form of alphabet, identifiable by its lack of fussy curves or flourishes.

Ruth James made a sampler with the inscription 'Westtown School' in this kind of plain lettering. She also embroidered a row of digits, two alphabets and the following verse:

> To crown both my age and my youth,
> Let me mark where religion has trod,
> Since nothing but virtue and truth
> Can reach to the throne of my God.

She enclosed this in the simplest of all oval borders, a line of straight stitches, and dated the piece 1800. Within a few years Westtown samplers contained as many as eight varieties of alphabet, the names of parents as well as verses all enclosed in wavy leaf-and-vine oval frames. Several stylized flower motifs might also be dotted around the piece.

In 1820 a sampler by Sarah James still contained the vine leaf border that was the school's signature, but it also featured a small landscape of a tree, a hill, some french knotted lambs, birds and butterflies. In the centre she had embroidered the names of all her immediate family, an extract of 'six lines of philosophical admonitions' as well as the name of her teacher. She enclosed the whole piece in fashionable silk quilling ribbon.

Both girls and boys were educated at these 'progressive' Friends schools, but only the girls learned needlework. At first they were taught basic plain sewing and would probably have made a darning sampler. American darning samplers were not common and those made at Quaker schools were far less attractively designed than the English variety. They were highly practical pieces, usually comprising six or eight but sometimes as many as twenty-five squares of sample repairs. The central unit frequently displayed simulated knitting in chain stitches.

When these techniques had been mastered, the girls might then make one of the silk globe covers for which the school is renowned. Ruth Wright made one of light blue silk with the longitudinal lines couched in blue silk and the tropics of Cancer and Capricorn in red silk. Some outlining was done in white silk with the lettering in black ink. These are often referred to as 'Globe' samplers and were similar in conception to the map samplers made in English schools. The latter never achieved great popularity in America although one or two examples are known, interesting more for their historical and geographical information than for the style of their embroidery. In April 1803, the United States virtually doubled its size by buying from the French the entire Mississippi Valley up to the Rocky Mountains. The area was one of the richest agricultural regions in the world. This immensely significant event prompted many needleworkers to turn their hands to maps. An outline of North

A terrestrial globe in silk with silk needlework, 1815.

*Samplers*

America, stamped on linen with the Louisiana Territory boldly delineated, was quickly produced expressly for needle-workers. One much later map sampler is of New York State embroidered by Elizabeth Ann Goldin in 1829. It is full of statistical information. For example, in neat lettering beneath PENNSYLVANIA she tells us that the population of New York State in the year she made the map was 1,392,812 and that 'Long Island is the most important Island belonging to the State of New York, 140 miles in length and from 10 to 15 broad, contains three counties and numerous flourishing towns, population 87,000.' She added: 'Lake Erie is the celebrated scene of Perry's victory over a British fleet, September 10th 1813 ... Lake Champlain is celebrated for the victory gained by Macdonough over a British fleet of far superior force, September, 1814.'

The samplers mentioned so far are notable in that they were almost all made at known schools. This enables us to see them in the context in which they were created. Several other American samplers fall quite clearly into groups which have not yet been given a name. There is a small collection of samplers made in Newport, Rhode Island, between 1770 and 1795 that share similar motifs, arrangement and style. Hannah Taylor's is possibly the best known of these but her elegant ladies and gentlemen, rows of alphabet, flowing floral border growing from urns, as well as the tablet at the bottom containing her name, birthday and the date of her sampler, are characteristics shared by others in the group. The teacher responsible for these layered designs is not known but several names have been suggested as possibilities.

Three samplers made by Susanna M. Holland in 1816, Ann E. England in 1820 and Eliza J. Benneson in 1835 all bear a remarkable resemblance to each other, as if they were copied from the same master pattern. This would explain both the similarities and the discrepancies between them. The wide outer borders contain several varieties of large, colourful blooms around an inner rectangle of a simple verse. Above and below the verse are alphabets and a small landscape. Eliza Benneson reflected:

> Let My few remaining days
> Be devoted to thy praise
> So the last, the closing scene
> Shall be tranquil and serene

It has been suggested that the school where these three were made was in Baltimore or Delaware.

There are many other regional characteristics which make it possible to group some American samplers; for example, bowknots hold-

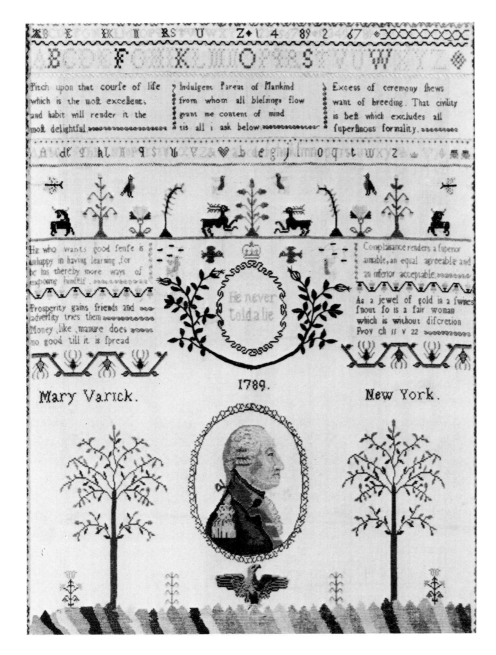

Mary Varick's 'Washington' sampler, New York, 1789, the year he assumed the presidency.

ing up swags of roses were a typical Connecticut hallmark. At the same time the persistence of English and European motifs is still noticeable. In particular it is surprising to see a number of American samplers bearing acorns and crowns, both of which could be said to be symbols of the monarchy against which, by 1775, Americans had engaged in battle. Of course, the crown motif may have been embroidered by a girl from a loyalist family or by a new arrival in America. But perhaps both crowns and acorns were as much decorative motifs without any deeper significance, just as they often were in the mother country. Another popular English and European subject seen in American samplers is pairs of birds, often peacocks, and these may owe their origins to Sibmacher's patterns. However, the ubiquity of Adam and Eve, the Tree of Knowledge and the Serpent is not altogether remarkable in a nation of Bible lovers.

The quintessential American symbol of patriotism from the revolutionary war onwards was the eagle with outstretched wings. Surprisingly, not many of these found their way on to samplers, and most that have survived were not worked until the nineteenth century. Mary Varick of New York managed to combine several different motifs. The focal point of her sampler was a medallion of George Washington with another medallion above this containing the words 'He never told a lie'. What could be more American than this portrait with an eagle standing proudly below? Yet in the very centre of her work Mary included a royal crown, a strange mixture indeed! She dated the piece 1789, the year Washington assumed the Presidency.

Sarah S. Caldwell, a South Carolina girl, also embroidered an eagle on her 1806 sampler, with a pennant flying from his beak calling for 'Independence'. Two quite similar samplers were made in Pennsylvania,

Margaret Moss's densely worked Pennsylvania sampler, 1825. Stylized border patterns, angels and stars, a grand American eagle and a pastoral landscape combine to create an imposing piece. The informality and individuality of the central section are very American in feeling, but the sampler is surrounded by a traditional English-style border.

both displaying resplendent eagles covered by shields and with another symbol of patriotism, American flags, in their claws. In 1825 eleven-year-old Margaret Moss put a streamer in the beak of hers bearing the words *E Pluribus Unum*. Near the top Margaret made cross-stitched angels and stars, which were derived from the continental sampler tradition. But then she let loose her imagination depicting a lively landscape with cows, sheep and shepherd, a red house, a beehive complete with swarming bees and children playing. Her own name and the date of the work appear in a wreath on one side with the name Elizabeth Wiert, aged 60 died 1825 (presumably her grandmother), in a memorial wreath on the opposite side. The other piece was made by Maria Bolen in 1816.

Not only the motifs, but sometimes the verses too were exactly those seen on English samplers, copied straight out of Reverend Isaac Watts' book. But often the poems had their own peculiarly American flavour and there was not the same insistence on rhyming couplets as in English sampler verses. For example, Mary Belcher in 1808 quoted the following:

> Love all, Trust a few
> Do wrong to none be able for thine enemy
> Rather in power than in use keep thy friend
> Under thy own life's key be check'd for silence
> But never talk for speech.

Patty Polk, a ten-year-old from Kent, Maryland, made no secret of her feelings about embroidery in 1800: 'Patty Polk did this and she hated every stitch she did in it. She loves to read much more.'

Sometimes samplers were made as presents for relatives in England and the inscription might include the following lines taken from an 1803 rhyme:

> No barrier Ocean can divide
> Affection's kindred love
> And that I've ne'er forgotten thee
> Let this Memento Prove.

Thirteen-year-old Ann Wing from Boston had a wry sense of humour:

> One did commend me to a WIFE both Fair and Young
> That had French Spanish and Italian Tongue
> I thankd him kindly and told him I loved none such
> For I thought one tongue For a Wife too much
> What love Ye not The Learned Yes as my Life
> A Learned Schollar but not a Learned Wife.

ABOVE Lucretia Bright worked a simple but charming tree for her family record of 1820. This is a well-known theme for genealogical samplers; at least four others are known to come from the Concord/Lexington, Massachusetts, area.

OPPOSITE The identity of the worker of this sampler is not known. Inscribed 'KA FA TW 1975', it was probably made in Chester County, Pennsylvania. The appeal of the piece lies partly in its charming lack of perspective, its fresh but subtle colouring and the gentle activity of the scene.

## Samplers

In 1833, Mary Eyre showed a man on bended knee in her sampler to illustrate some lines entitled 'The converted Indian's Prayer'.

> In de dark wood no Indian nigh
> Den me look heaven and send up cry.
> Upon my knee so low,
> Dal god so high a shiny place.
> See me in night with teary face.
> My priest do tell me so.
> He send his angel take me care
> He comes his self and hear my prayer.
> If Indian heart do pray.

After about 1800 certain forms of American sampler became more prevalent. The family record or register, a favourite in the eighteenth century, increased in popularity. The names of dead relatives were usually embroidered in black silk to contrast with others worked in bright colours. Spaces were often left for deaths to be recorded at a later date. In the first decades of the nineteenth century the genealogical sampler was sometimes made in the style of an actual tree, with each name taking up a separate fruit. Lucretia Bright from Watertown, Massachusetts, made her family record in this way, framing her tree within a three-sided border of trailing roses. The base of the tree was covered by two hearts, clearly referring to her parents, who according to the sampler were married on 27 December 1797. The births of six daughters and one son were recorded and it is interesting that the arrival of the first daughter, Susan, on 20 June 1798 was reported as factually as the rest.

These family records were not usually as decorative as other samplers but often included pillars at the side and possibly an arch over the top. They supply interesting sociological information, such as that second and third marriages appear to have been quite common. Eliza Ann Hunt in her sampler of 1824 entwined three hearts, one containing her father's name, a second shared by her mother and stepmother, with a third heart inverted and on a lower level recording both marriages.

Many of these genealogies record the deaths of young siblings. But mourning samplers in their own right became especially popular at the turn of the century, prompted largely by the death in 1799 of the young nation's first great hero, George Washington. Often made on satin, these pieces would usually include both painting and embroidery and might use human hair. Other typical features were at least one weeping willow shading a doleful young girl in her grief, possibly visiting a tomb or an urn. The girl would probably be dressed in a loose, flowing robe

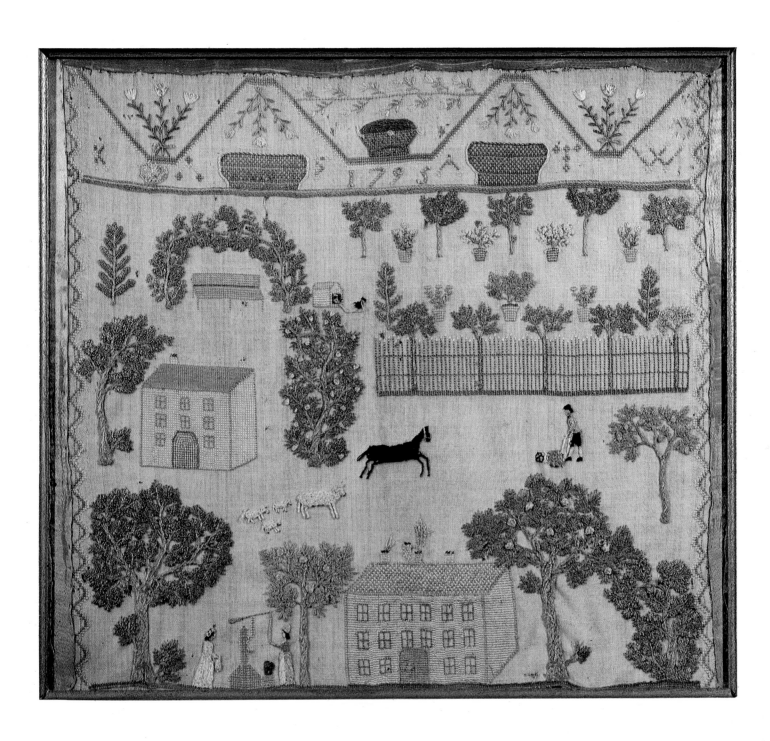

## America's Blossoming Tradition

reflecting the pervading neo-classicism of the early nineteenth century. These pieces unashamedly exuded sentimentality, but were considered the height of good taste at this time. Even schoolgirls were expected to indulge.

Mary V. Wilson of Trenton, New Jersey, was just nine when in 1828 she made her mourning sampler of embroidery in silk and metallic thread with some watercolour and silk appliqué. Her scene of a young woman weeping beside a willow-shrouded urn with Washington's home, Mount Vernon, in the background, was derived from a contemporary engraving by Samuel Seymour called 'In Memory of General Washington and his Lady'. It was a popular practice to copy engravings in this way and there were several versions of Mount Vernon on a gentle hillside. Margaret Barnholt, a Pennsylvania girl, included a small mourning scene to the right of her otherwise very gay and busy sampler. She pictured a man, woman, boy and girl standing around a tomb upon which are the initials R W and E B, with the verse:

Mother dear weep not for me
When in this yard my grave you see
My time was short and blest was he
That called me to eternity.

Perhaps EB refers to a brother or sister and RW to a cousin.

There were a few lacework samplers made in America, mostly in the Philadelphia region, in the late eighteenth century. They are reminiscent of the exquisite cut- and drawnwork samplers of seventeenth-century England, but they display a peculiarly American flavour. This is chiefly because they were made in the form of well-designed pictures instead of featuring several rows or bands of different techniques. The most popular design was a basket of flowers – in fact, this was a favourite American motif in several needlework forms – with the stems outlined usually in chain stitch and the blooms filled in with drawn- or Dresden work. Worked in white silk or linen thread on a fine linen or cotton fabric, the technique of Dresden work required that several warp and weft threads be cut away; the remaining threads were embroidered together into lacey stitches. Sometimes the background fabrics were so fine the threads could simply be pulled together without any being removed. These lacework samplers often included squares containing examples of cutwork such as hollie point. In 1771, Jane Humphreys made one of the most beautiful openwork compositions: a Dresden work flower basket filled the centre but she also made ten squares and circles of cutwork down two of the outside edges, with several other smaller ones scattered around the piece.

Each of these family records includes the conventions of side pillars and an arch above, yet they are completely different in mood.

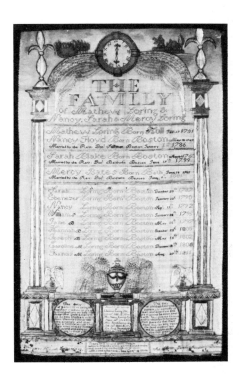

OPPOSITE A representation of the central block of Inveraray Castle is the focal point of this magnificent sampler, worked in coloured silks on wool in 1822. The verse is part of a hymn written by Bishop Thomas Ken in 1709.

## America's Blossoming Tradition

A small group of samplers that deserves a brief mention are those made by American Jewish girls in the mid-nineteenth century. Jewish families tended to live in cities or large towns and so the samplers they made were, on the whole, within the American mainstream. But it is possible to recognize one or two of them from the inclusion of either a Hebrew alphabet and one or two Jewish religious symbols or a reliable family history. For example, one made by Rachel Seixas in New York City c. 1830 is in most respects a typical early American sampler of silk embroidery on linen with a floral border enclosing a verse; but Rachael's Jewish ancestry is well known. Others depict two chairs either side of a table, which is thought to be the Sabbath table, and a representation of the Sabbath lamp. An 1817 sampler signed 'Zirle' contains a cityscape that, although not very accurate, is thought to be Jerusalem, with the dominant building probably symbolizing the Holy Temple. In addition to the Hebrew alphabet, and the table and chairs, this sampler also bears a motif with a long ancestry in Protestant European samplers – the spies from Canaan carrying a bunch of grapes. In Christian iconography the grapes become wine to symbolize the blood of Jesus, but in Jewish tradition this motif signifies the Holy Land. The provenance of this sampler is unknown but the general tone suggests that Dutch or German origins are more likely than American.

As America grew, so did the tradition of sampler-making. Students from some of the best academies would go off to new schools spreading the techniques they had learned. Young children in the West made the same sort of alphabet samplers that their New England cousins had made a hundred years before. But whereas New England schoolchildren of the mid-eighteenth century would graduate from this to a more elaborate and delicate pictorial sampler, by the mid-nineteenth century an alphabet sampler in wool on a coarse canvas might be the only kind a young girl made. For by that time there was a general decline in American samplers – caused partly by the new craze for Berlin woolwork, which had taken an equally strong hold in Britain, and partly by the insistence on a better academic education for women.

ABOVE A nineteenth-century Jewish American sampler, worked by Bek Berta in polychrome wool on an undyed cotton canvas.

OPPOSITE Suzannah Razor's lovely and delicate sampler of 1783 contains examples of both Dresden work and hollie point.

# 5
# The Nineteenth Century

Throughout the English-speaking world the nineteenth century has come to be known as the Victorian Age. The Queen who ascended the British throne at the tender age of eighteen has been blamed for the rigid standards of morality and decency which marked her reign, yet at the same time she has been praised for the great achievements of some of her bold and imaginative subjects and the prosperity of the nation as a whole. Victoria's reign witnessed immense changes in the political, social and economic climates in Britain. Paradoxically, it was an age that prided itself on its individualistic and *laissez-faire* attitudes and yet which saw more regulations and control by the central government than ever before. The influence of eighteenth-century English radicalism coupled with the spread of French and American revolutionary ideals made the general impetus towards reform strongest in the '30s and '40s, but the Chartist Movement for political reform and a wave of revolutions abroad in 1848 gave a new emphasis to reforming zeal in the latter part of the century.

The first step may have been the reform of Parliament in 1832, but it was the Poor Law Amendment Act two years later which introduced nearly all the administrative machinery to be used by the government later in the century. A Commission was established to enquire into the old Poor Law, a Central Committee of audit was set up and a Central Inspectorate was organized to enforce this and other Acts. This bureaucratic structure could be adapted for dealing with such problems as the inhumane conditions in the factories and mines, the burgeoning railway system that was the country's pride and joy, and the inadequate schooling that became a preoccupation among almost all classes and political parties in the nineteenth century.

OPPOSITE An alphabet, house, coronets, birds, animal, tree and flower motifs, all within a floral border, combine to make a well organized sampler worked in 1815 as a tribute to the embroideress' parents.

*Samplers*

In the wake of rapid industrialization, and as the traditional source of income from the land was being eroded, many of the country's poor were becoming destitute while the gentry were losing both status and power to the new manufacturers. At the same time the population of Great Britain was growing apace from 10.4 million in 1801, the first year of the official census, to 18.5 million in 1841, and much of the growth was concentrated in the new urban ghettos, areas where the middle-class industrialists and their families were learning rarely to venture.

Those who were able to seize the chances offered by industrialization were artisans, who found their skills were in increasing demand. They could move from town to town and often employed other men to work for them. Many of these skilled labourers rose to swell the ranks of the middle classes and could well become manufacturers and factory owners themselves. There was enough mobility to give credence to the prevailing opinion that poverty was often a spur to greater things, though this belief was softened by two factors. The first was that the religious consciences of a number of prominent persons helped ensure the passage of a large body of legislation aimed at controlling, if not actually improving, the lot of the working classes. Secondly, the increase in population meant that there were many more children to teach, while the concentration of so many adults in confined spaces resulted in the speedy dissemination of new and radical ideas. Together, these ensured that the educational question was in the forefront of the public consciousness.

It was inevitable that the ruling classes wanted control over the sort of education which should be given to the masses. But the working classes now also took an interest in the matter, equally captivated by the importance of education for themselves as much as for their children. William Lovett, a cabinet-maker who had become a prominent Chartist, recounted in his autobiography (1876) how he was first stimulated to intellectual enquiry after being introduced to a small literary association of working men. 'In short, my mind seemed to be awakened to a new mental existence: new feelings, hopes and aspirations sprang up within me and every spare moment was devoted to the acquisition of some kind of useful knowledge.'

Many of the schools for poor children at the beginning of the century had grown up from Sunday Schools, and even though the instruction was now extended to weekdays, the curriculum was only barely expanded beyond Bible-reading, social indoctrination and useful tasks. One such school was run by Hannah More, who described her system as follows: 'My plan of instruction is extremely simple and limited. They learn on weekdays such coarse works as may fit them for servants. I allow of no writing for the poor . . .' The children were evidently taught knitting, spinning and obedience – all that was considered necessary for them.

In spite of the new interest in education, school attendance was low throughout most of the century. Times were hard, and for most urban and rural children it was more important that they earned money sweeping chimneys, hauling coal or pulling turnips. Compulsory state-

Conditions in many nineteenth-century schools were cramped, and facilities inadequate. An entire school might be staffed by only one qualified teacher, who would enlist the help of pupil-teachers from among the older students.

*Samplers*

financed education seemed a long way off to the children of the early nineteenth century. But by 1870 an Education Act had been passed containing at least an explicit commitment to a national system of elementary schools and the machinery to implement them.

There was one alternative occupation for the girl who dreaded the thought of spending the rest of her days in a grimy factory – she could go into service with a family. The Victorian age saw a proliferation of domestic servants of both sexes on a previously unknown scale. Any well-to-do establishment would employ a pair of liveried footmen, a young lady's maid, several cooks and neat parlour maids and perhaps also a sewing maid, butler and valet. For many ladies, having the largest possible household of staff was the surest means of being considered genteel.

These new ladies of nineteenth-century society were expected to concern themselves with child-bearing, hand work, crafts, the management of their maids, religion, and voluntary activities. As the system became more firmly entrenched, a woman's importance in the home was extolled and glorified. This had the effect of delaying the academic instruction of women for decades so that, ultimately, both mistress and maid were the losers.

An important task of many a domestic servant – even if not specifically designated a 'sewing maid' – was to mark and repair household napery and clothes. This was why so many of the new schools for poor children, far from dispensing with the sampler as a piece of elaborate sewing from a bygone age, developed it for the new needs of their charges. Samplers made at the Bristol orphanages have survived in relatively large numbers and are excellent examples of this development. These pieces are usually worked on linen in black or red thread, or both, and contain several varieties of alphabets and numerals as well as perhaps eighty half rows of simple border patterns all worked in cross stitch. In the centre a Bible was usually represented with a small crucifix or two at the bottom. A moralistic verse might also be added. Many included a row of three-figure numbers which were probably identity tags for the girls. This practice was not confined to orphanages: several nineteenth-century schools are known to have used identity numbers too. Sometimes as many as twenty varieties of alphabet would be embroidered by orphanage girls, ranging from large capitals to minuscule lower-case letters. According to *The Workwoman's Guide* of 1837, the upright alphabet was most commonly used, while the Italian or sloping letters were required on fine linen such as handkerchiefs. The pieces were usually not only signed and dated but an address was included too. For example:

## The Nineteenth Century

MA Tipper
New Orphan House
North Wing
Ashley Down
Bristol
1808

ABOVE M A Tipper's densely worked sampler, 1808. More than any other examples, those pieces made in orphanages show the functional aspect of samplers as practice grounds for learning to mark household linen.

The general style of the orphanage samplers was extreme neatness and plainness with a strict economy of space. Not an inch of the linen was left unworked. Girls trained there would obviously be equipped to mark household items of all types with a very high standard of workmanship.

A full account of the importance of needlework in nineteenth-century schools is to be found in a book published 'by direction of the Commissioners of National Education in Ireland, 1853' and entitled *Simple Directions in Needle-work and Cutting out; intended for the use of the National Female Schools of Ireland. To which are added Specimens of work executed by the pupils of The Female National Model School*. With as many as seventy pupils per class it was obviously helpful to have clear guidelines set out for handling the lessons. The introductory remarks to the book explained:

The practical knowledge of needlework, with its appendages of cutting out and repairing &c., &c., must be regarded as very useful to all females, but particularly so to those of the humbler classes, whether applied to domestic purposes, or as a mode of procuring remunerative employment.

... It will be a useful practice to have the directions for each class read out for the children by its Monitress on one or two days of the week and to have the pupils questioned on occasions on the substance ... The simplicity of these arrangements, and their easy adaptation to the management of large numbers, have recommended them to very general adoption.

The children were taught marking by the eighth class, after learning tucking, trimming and buttonholing but before darning and herringboning, knitting and, of course, lacework. The manual said:

Marking in cross stitch, though very much superseded by the use of marking ink, is yet sufficiently useful, and is still so generally practised as to render a knowledge of the proper mode of doing it an indispensable part of the business of a National School for teaching plain-work.

The book went on to advise that, in addition to marking, the children of class eight could also be taught hem stitch by means of a sampler 'as the openness of the canvas renders it particularly convenient for that purpose'. Detailed instructions for making a sampler then followed:

BELOW Jane Humphreys, working in 1838, chose to show a ship going past the Menai Bridge in Wales – an unusually pictorial theme for the time. At the bottom of her sampler she included a few pertinent statistics, and acknowledged her teacher, Mrs Williams.

117

## Samplers

1. After seeing that the sampler is cut evenly, lay the hem down, *exactly to a thread*, and according to the rules for articles having four sides.

2. Draw a thread or two close under the hem, on each of the sides; then, having sewed the end of the turn, begin to hem-stitch.

3. Pass the needle under two threads, and draw it; then put it back, *across the same threads*, and out through the edge of the hem; this forms the stitch. Muslin or cambric requires to have a great number of threads drawn; and also a greater number taken in each stitch.

4. When the sampler is hemmed, begin the letters, leaving two or four threads between the upper part of the letter and the edge of the hem, and if a row is worked, observe the same rule.

5. To form the stitch, take two threads each way; put the needle in at the right hand *upper* corner of these, and passing it *aslant* under them, bring it out at the left hand *lower* corner; then put the needle in as before, but bring it out *straight* towards you; and, thirdly, set in one stitch across.

6. Leave eighteen threads between each row of the coarse sampler; but when marking finer material, the distance must be regulated agreeably to taste.

7. Begin each letter separately, and work in the end of thread with the *first two* stitches. The thread should be fastened off, on the wrong side, at the end of each letter, and not carried on from one to another.

8. Leave two or four threads between each letter or figure of a sampler; but when marking shirts, cravats, or house-linen, eight or ten threads will be necessary.

9. The straight letters are the first taught, then the slanting, and lastly the round. The second sampler may contain the letters in their regular order, then the small letters and the figures up to 10. When the small letters can be correctly worked, Bolton may be used.

The book also spoke about 'taking in plain work' if it became necessary to provide funds for the support of a school. Evidently it was a common practice for some schools to accept repair work. A Norfolk School log-book for 1862 recounts how the local Rector had much influence at the establishment: 'Girls put Needlework to practical account today by darning and mending worn linen from the rectory – the finished work was sent to the rectory but sometimes it was sent back again.'

And so in the nineteenth century English samplers generally were little more than a school exercise preparing the girls for these sorts of essential household tasks. They so lacked in originality that it was possible for precise instructions about making them to appear in the thorough *Dictionary of Needlework* by Sophia F. Caulfeild and Blance L. Saward in 1882.

Beneath the heading 'To Make A Sampler', the dictionary advised as follows:

Jesie Balfour's 1828 sampler has many paired initials at top and bottom. Other traditional motifs include Adam and Eve, detached birds, animals, flowers and trees, and a strawberry border.

Take some Mosaic Canvas, of the finest make, and woven so that each thread is at an equal distance apart. Cut this 18 inches wide and 20 inches long, and measure off a border all round of 4 inches. For the border, half an inch from the edge, draw out threads in a pattern to the depth of half an inch, and work over these with coloured silk; then work a conventional scroll pattern, in shades of several colours, and in TENT STITCH, to fill up the remaining 3 inches of the border. Divide the centre of the Sampler into three sections. In the top section work a figure design. (In the old Samplers this was generally a sacred subject, such as Adam and Eve before the Tree of Knowledge.) In the centre section work an Alphabet in capital letters, and in the bottom an appropriate verse, the name of the worker, and the date.

The nineteenth-century school samplers relied on a number of small pattern books intended for children and especially printed for the purpose. One of the most popular was a miniature volume entitled *The Embroidery*

## Samplers

*and Alphabet Sampler Book*, which included a large choice of animals, ships, houses, alphabets, numerals, floral patterns, and even girls' forenames. Another pamphlet, published in 1806 'for the use of schools' contained ten varieties of alphabets including German text, Old English, Roman print, and Italian print. Eliza Amelia Sands even added half a row of punctuation marks – & , ; : ? ! – all in cross stitch, to her 1830 sampler. This was reproduced, no doubt, directly from an English grammar book.

If samplers were not copied from pattern books, they might be reproductions of a master pattern worked by a pupil–teacher. The system of pupil–teachers was an absolute necessity with classes of such large numbers and pleased the Victorians both for its economy and because it offered a small amount of social mobility for bright children of limited means. Some pupil–teachers are known to have reached the rank of Schools Commissioner. Samplers signed by pupil–teachers are rare, but Eliza Sophia Newton made one in 1808 comprising a map of Norfolk with the county divided into 'hundreds'. After her name she embroidered 'pupil teacher, 1st year'. The map is thought to have been made for the children to copy.

In general, school samplers did not differ dramatically from those of the late eighteenth century; some motifs, such as twin birds, stags, a parrot on a spray and fruit trees, and border patterns of strawberries and honeysuckle, were little changed even from the sixteenth and seventeenth centuries. More buildings made an appearance in the nineteenth century: sometimes these were representations of the worker's home or school, but more often they were copied from an embroidery picture book. Many of the elongated structures were headed Solomon's Temple. The name of the school was mentioned more frequently than before. And domestic animals such as dogs, cats and horses often featured in the later pieces.

Most of the favourite verses were still taken from Reverend Isaac Watts' songbook. But perhaps the most popular sampler verse of all was one which has not yet been found on a sampler before 1794 and is therefore thought not to have been written by him. Several different versions of this verse are known, but eleven-year-old Martha Glazebrook's was typical:

> Jesus permit thy gracious name to stand,
> As the first effort of an infant hand,
> And while her finger's [*sic*] on the canvas move
> Engage her tender heart to seek thy love.

Helen Gibson used a quotation from Genesis above her representation of Adam and Eve. Worked *c.* 1825 in coloured silks on wool, this sampler is a good example of early nineteenth-century style.

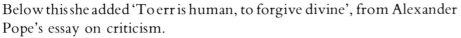

LEFT Castles set in a country scene were popular in nineteenth-century samplers. Sarah Morgan's picture of Penrhyn Castle in North Wales was probably copied from a lithograph; the castle is also reproduced on a Berlin woolwork picture in the National Museum of Wales.

BELOW Like multiplication samplers, those containing pounds, shillings and pence charts proved valuable *aide-memoires* to industrious students. This decorative piece was worked by E. Sherwin in 1835.

Below this she added 'To err is human, to forgive divine', from Alexander Pope's essay on criticism.

Nineteenth-century school samplers were made almost exclusively in cross stitch, often in wool instead of silk, on a coarse mesh canvas. Cross stitch, which in this century became known as sampler stitch, was quite useful for large amounts of lettering with little decoration and lent itself well, for example, to the multiplication charts in vogue at that time. In 1827 Sarah Grace, beneath the heading 'Multiplication', stitched a chart for the twelve-times table. Using only red thread for the piece, she also included a homily on virtue, a row of coronets and an alphabet. It is quite possible that Sarah was Scottish as three other similar charts are known, all with Scottish connections. One was by Margaret Gray, c. 1820–40, another by Jean Miller, c. 1825 and the third was inscribed 'JE Multiplication table M', c. 1850–60. This was the least useful piece as the worker calculated that twelve times eleven was one hundred and twenty-three.

One school in which a particularly original type of sampler was made was a Quaker Friends school in Ackworth, Yorkshire, founded in 1779. Some of the surviving Ackworth school samplers were made in the late

Frances Rae worked her Ackworth School sampler in silks of different colours. On the back of another surviving sampler from the school is a notice which says: 'Such Girls as choose to have one of these [samplers] work them in playhours as it is thought it would take up too much time to do them in School, having other Pieces to work, as well as their own and the Household linen to make and mend.'

eighteenth century, others in the early nineteenth. Worked entirely in cross stitch usually in monochrome silks on a woollen background, these contained a series of medallions, garlands and motifs with a border of half medallions or half motifs. Some of the garlands contained initials, a date or a motto. Mary Gregory worked one of this type in 1807 in brown silks with several pairs of birds and flowers encircled in her neatly spaced tablet patterns. In one she embroidered MG to EG 1807, in another MM 1807, in a third 'A token of love', in a fourth MG to MT, with LB, AG and MS in others. She did not name Ackworth school. Francis Rae made a similar one in 1797 which did name Ackworth, M. Quertier worked one in 1799 and Eliza Trusted, signed ET, in 1803. Some of the motifs in these examples are identical, others are very similar. Many of them are exactly those used on the tiny pincushions that were such popular nineteenth-century gifts. Mary Gregory was unlikely to have

been making her sampler as a gift for EG, MT, MM and all the others.
But perhaps she was practising the patterns she would use on pincushions
for these people. There is known to exist a knitted pincushion made by
a member of ET's family which contains a pattern identical to one on
her sampler and the initials ES. Another pincushion in the same style
from the same family has 'From Ackworth School' on the reverse.

It is interesting that the only other schools where samplers with similar
types of motifs are known to have been made were the Quaker schools
in America. Although the girls at Westtown School in Pennsylvania and
its sister school in New York, the Nine Partners Boarding School, did
not specialize in the floral and geometric medallions that characterized
Ackworth samplers, several examples exist. Jane Merritt's of 1803, which
was executed while she attended the Nine Partners School, contained
some fifteen stylized floral motifs with a border of sixteen half tablets and
one corner tablet all in exactly the same Ackworth style.

As the links between Westtown and Ackworth were, from the beginning, extremely close, it is not altogether surprising to find the same
type of sampler being made on both sides of the Atlantic. A large number
of Philadelphia Friends were travelling to England, mostly on religious
missions, in the last years of the nineteenth century. All of them visited
Ackworth and entries in their diaries and letters supply abundant evidence of their interest in founding a school along similar lines in America.
A major step was taken in 1790 when Owen Biddle, a prominent Friend,
published a pamphlet entitled: 'A plan for a School on an Establishment
similar to that of Ackworth in Yorkshire, Great Britain, varied to suit
the circumstances of the Youth within the limits of the Yearly Meeting
for Pennsylvania and New Jersey.' It was this plan which was accepted.

Most Friends in the Philadelphia region were familiar in some detail
not only with the daily programme and religious training of Ackworth
students but also with all the rules and regulations of the school. They
would doubtless also have had a thorough knowledge of how Ackworth
girls learned needlework. It is known that at least one sampler was made
by a student at Ackworth and presented in 1788 to Rebecca Jones, later
a member of the first Westtown Committee. Although this was not in
the particular style associated with Ackworth it is quite likely that others
which were, were sent over as gifts. In this way it would have been natural
to have copied the style.

The pervading sense of gloom and doom, already present in eighteenth-
century samplers, hardly diminished in the nineteenth-century pieces.
Several young children embroidered just one line, 'Live to die', on their
alphabet samplers. But Margaret Morgan, a pupil at the Westbrook

An unusual harbour scene by
Euphemia Doieg, 1814. She probably
based her illustration on a print.

## Samplers

School in Wales, put into words the fears of many of her peers in the following verse at the top of a glorious pictorial sampler:

> There is an hour when I must die.
> Nor can I tell how soon twill come.
> A thousand children young as I,
> Are calld by death to hear their doom.

This verse, written by Dr Watts, was surrounded by a border of honeysuckle, pansies and roses. Below it Margaret included three beautifully worked biblical scenes of Elijah being fed by the ravens, Moses in the Bullrushes, and the Flight into Egypt. But in the middle of these traditional motifs she highlighted contemporary achievement by displaying a hot-air balloon with two passengers and a flag on either side.

With death an all-pervasive reality, a homily on the virtues of health is not surprising. In 1814, M. Fennah embroidered this verse on her sampler:

> Health Seems a Cherub Most Divinely bright,
> More soft than Air, More gay than Morning Light,
> Hail, blooming Goddess, thou propitious power,
> Whose blessings Mortals Next to Life implore,
> Such Graces in your Heavenly Eyes appear
> That Cottages are Courts, when you are there.

As in America, the early years of the nineteenth century saw a vogue in Britain for memorial or mourning samplers. Just as the death of George Washington had prompted the fashion in the United States, so in England the death in 1817 of young Princess Charlotte, daughter of George IV, had the same effect. The princess, who was 22 when she died during childbirth, was the heir to the British throne. The English mourning pieces utilized many of the traditional elements such as weeping willows, urns and tablets and some also added beadwork. Elizabeth Davey Catchpole made her memorial sampler almost entirely in beaded floral designs. In a panel beneath the word SACRED, she embroidered:

> To the memory of William Davey Privat Soldier
> 94 Regiment of foot who was slain at the
> Glorious battle of Cannanore [sic] East Indie
> July 25 1839 aged 27 years.

One sampler commemorating a death is, however, a puzzle. Sewn in coloured silks on linen, the piece contains floral motifs, birds and butterflies, a crown and two verses with two medallions in the lower half. Inside one medallion is the name Martha Grant, 1833 aged ten years.

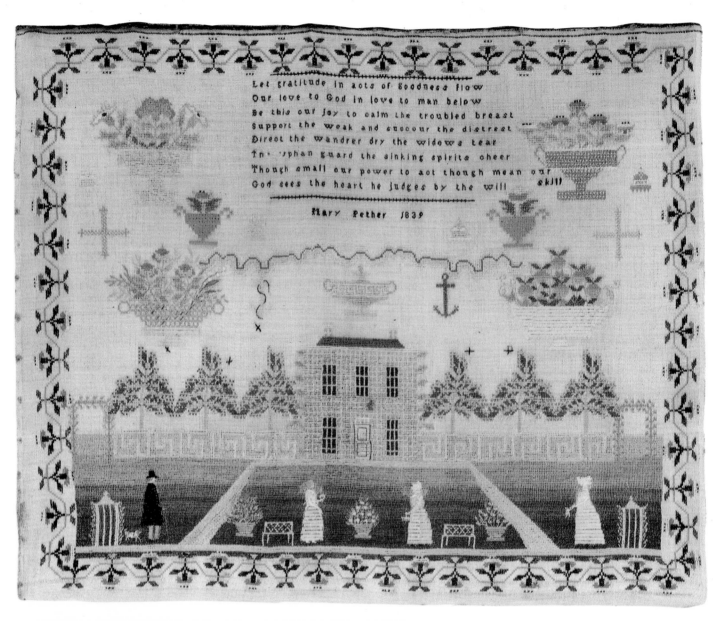

Let gratitude in acts of goodness flow
Our love to God in love to man below
Be this our joy to calm the troubled breast
Support the weak and succour the distrest
Direct the wandrer dry the widows tear
In orphan guard the sinking spirits cheer
Though small our power to act though mean our skill
God sees the heart he judges by the will

Mary Pether 1839

## The Nineteenth Century

The other contains the words 'Departed this life Oct 31ᵗ 1834 Aged 11 years'. There is no apparent difference in technique visible in the needlework. If Martha worked the sampler but left it unfinished, whose name was she planning to put in the second cartouche? If a relative worked the whole piece in memory of Martha, why did she not sign it?

There is a small group of samplers concerned with death in a rather specific way. These were made by people who believed in the Second Coming of Christ. There were a number of Millenarial movements in England from the 1790s onwards which found an especially receptive audience among the poor and dispossessed of the industrial North and Midlands. The passion of hundreds of working men and women in these towns was waiting to be tapped by charismatic preachers who appeared at open-air public lectures. Some movements also printed newsheets to explain their views. The *Second Advent Harbinger*, published in Bristol and later in Maidenhead in 1844, was one of these written by adherents of the American adventist, William Miller. Several slogans that appeared in this broadsheet have also been noted on samplers of the period. And so, a movement which rarely finds a mention in history books has been recorded in needlework. A favourite Millerite slogan was 'Prepare to meet thy God', a verse taken from the Book of Amos. The Millerites took this phrase as their own and believed it meant they were to be ready for the Second Coming of Jesus in 1844. A sampler made in Cotgrave, Nottingham, by Louisa Ann Morris in May 1843 is inscribed:

> Prepare to meet your God
> That heaven may be your home.

Several others that all say 'Prepare to meet thy God' and were made between 1825 and 1850 have also been noted.

The Second Advent Movement specifying a time of Christ's reappearance was eventually disappointed. 1844 and then 1847 – the suggestion of another school of thought – both passed uneventfully. One sampler dated 1848 by fourteen-year-old Mary Ann Watson is inscribed:

> And the Lord direct your hearts into the
> Love of God and into the patient waiting for Christ.

a quotation from the Second Book of Corinthians which probably indicates a reluctance to abandon a belief that had meant so much.

In fact, religion as such, other than in a general moralistic sense, rarely found its way on to samplers, and crucifixes were especially rare on British examples. Ten-year-old Hannah Kemp's sampler of 1823 contained a picture of Christ on the Cross with the following verse:

OPPOSITE Sampler and detail by Mary Pether, 1839, worked in Algerian eye, cross and satin stitches on a woollen canvas. Crowns, anchors and baskets of flowers are included in this lovely country scene.

Many buildings shown on nineteenth-century British samplers were called Solomon's Temple; the inclusion of a crucifix, however, was rare.

His sacred limbs they stretch they tear
With nails they fasten to the wood
His sacred limbs expos'd and bare
Or only cover'd with his blood.

This amount of realistic detail was rare. Although Victorian women were concerned with a public display of religion, voluntary work and church-going were all that was required. Hannah Kemp also included a representation of Solomon's Temple in her piece and this popular building, or a short Bible extract, was generally considered sufficient to add a serious tone to a sampler.

The verse Lucy Grant chose was in keeping with the way religious sentiment was usually expressed in samplers. She embroidered:

> Father whateer of earthly bliss.
> Thy sovreign will denies.
> Accepted at thy throne of grace.
> Let this petition rise.
>
> Give me a calm a thankful heart.
> From every murmur free.
> The blessings of thy grace impart.
> And make me live to thee.

Lucy made her sampler in 1840 in Regent Town, Sierra Leone, one of a few examples which illustrate how completely British morals and educational standards were exported to the colonies. The verses were taken from a hymn by Ann Steele published in 1760.

Some young children were given only a large extract from the Bible to include in their samplers, which lent a sombre air to these pieces. Possibly the best known of this type are those made by the Brontë sisters, Charlotte in April 1829, aged thirteen, Emily Jane in March 1829, aged eleven and Anne in January 1830, aged ten. Worked in greenish-black silk on rough canvases, the pieces are totally without ornament apart from a Greek key border, each one the same, rather melancholy. Although plain and undecorative, these are fascinating pieces when seen in the context of the bleakness of the land round the Haworth parsonage in Yorkshire where they lived, and the tragedies that had three times struck their family. One can easily imagine that the words of the Proverbs stitched on the three samplers had been instilled into the hardworking children to help them through difficult times.

More pitiable than sombre was a sampler containing a long inscription of religious verse made by a woman prisoner in Bedford jail for the Governor's daughter. It is signed 'Annie Parker. Done by her with her own hair, June 82'. Below this she has embroidered: 'Presented by her to Miss D. A. Roberts', with a heart either side and a crucifix in the middle. A small band added to the linen sampler has the words 'We hope to meet again.' In addition to hair, the work includes some silk thread and crochet cotton worked around the edge. It was very finely executed, mostly in cross stitch but with the panels of linen hemmed and outlined with feather and double feather stitch. A similar piece was made in 1879 by a woman prisoner called Ellen Parker, also known as Annie Parker, a confirmed alcoholic who went to prison at least fifty times for drunkenness. The second sampler was made during one such term when she

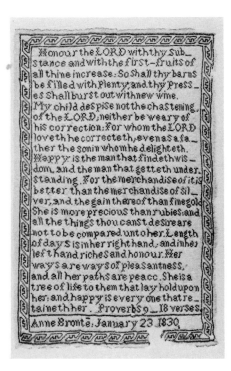

A Greek key border surrounds an otherwise unadorned extract from Proverbs, worked by Anne Brontë in 1830.

*Samplers*

Like those by Ellen and Annie Parker, this sampler was worked in human hair. By an anonymous prisoner, 1879.

struck up a friendship with her cell mate, also an alcoholic, who had with her a small baby. Apparently Ellen Parker helped nurse the infant through an illness and the grateful mother begged a keepsake of her as a reminder of this kindness. Ellen made a sampler with her own hair stitched upon a headscarf – all the materials she had at hand. The two pieces are similar in so many respects that it is almost inconceivable they were not made by the same person. Ellen Parker died in 1884.

Gift samplers, usually small, ornamental pieces, were popular throughout the nineteenth century. In 1879 'B.L.' included a hymn and inscription as well as several patterns of horizontal borders, plants, crowns and hearts. She signed it:

> Alberta Hubbard
> a gift from her cousin B.L.
> May 31st 1879

Other samplers were made not as gifts but to commemorate the work of notable individuals or historical events. The end of the Napoleonic Wars in 1814 was one such landmark which Elizabeth Rooke celebrated in her needlework. She signed herself as a pupil of Market Bosworth

130

Boarding School, Leicestershire, believed to be an early co-educational establishment. Below a prose quotation on religion appears a magnificent shield bedecked with tasselled drapes and topped by a sparkling crown. Elizabeth went to great trouble to create an imposing sampler and used coloured silk threads and some yellow chenille in cross, long and short, stem, satin and couching stitches and french knots. She embellished her work with applied green and white silk, partly padded, and cream silk braid, touches rarely seen in English samplers. Within the shield she inscribed: 'Signed at Paris by the ALLIED Sovereigns May 30th 1814,' and above 'PEACE RATIFIED, FRENCH SATISFIE(D) THE PEOPLE GRATIFIED.'

Susannah Bradshaw's slave sampler, worked in coloured wools with a floral border, 1853.

When Susannah Bradshaw made a black slave in chains the centre of her sampler in November 1853, she may have had in mind the publication in America the previous year of Harriet Beecher Stowe's *Uncle Tom's Cabin*. She embroidered two winged cherubs to watch over her slave and in large letters at the top of her piece worked 'LIVE AND LET LIVE'.

The nineteenth century saw several new types of sampler, some of which were a consequence of the increasing industrialization of the textile industry. There exists a small group of samplers with needle-made lace patterns darned on a machine-made net background. Although these are neither signed nor dated, manufactured net was not made until the early 1800s. The period also witnessed the introduction of trade samplers. Wives of miners or factory workers, for example, could supplement their families' meagre incomes by accepting fine sewing work to be done at home, using trade samplers as master patterns. The work would then be returned to a factory for completion.

These outworkers were perhaps the group who suffered most from the industrial revolution. Their wages were kept low on the basis that if they were paid any more the money would be frittered away on 'weekly debauches', but mostly they lacked organization to press their claims. The hand of the manufacturer was strengthened further as the ranks of the poor and unemployed in industrial northern Britain grew during the early nineteenth century, swelled by unemployed agricultural workers, Irish immigrants and demobilized soldiers.

One example of outwork which needed a sampler was adding the 'clocks', or ornamental embroidered finishes to the leg and instep of knitted socks and stockings and occasionally to gloves and mittens. According to Caulfeild and Saward's dictionary, the clocks were worked in either filoselle or silk 'of a colour that either matches or contrasts the stocking they adorn . . . they are embroidered before the foot is knitted and after

## Samplers

An early nineteenth-century sampler, probably Scottish, worked in white cotton and linen on cotton.

the heel is finished. The name given to this decoration is considered to have originated in resemblance to the pendulum of a clock.'

The work, sometimes known as chevening, was usually distributed to the women by an agent of the manufacturer. He would give out the stockings for the next week's work – some women taking as many as three dozen pairs – and pay for the last week's work. The patterns, embroidered in satin stitch, were copied from a sampler on stocking web, using the woven loops of the fabric as a guide. However, a fall in the demand for the splendid hose of the eighteenth century, together with the introduction of machinery that could add the clocks, gradually stifled this cottage industry.

Commercial samplers were also needed for the delicate floral embroidery on muslin known as Ayrshire work, or sewed muslin, which flourished from about 1820–70. Ayrshire embroidery was made in a wide range of naturalistic floral patterns and trails influenced by the imported Indian cottons. Worked mostly in satin or stem stitch in white cotton on white muslin with some spaces cut out and filled with needlepoint lace, the finished product was in demand for babies' as well as ladies' clothes, men's shirt frills, and handkerchiefs. Although it was called Ayrshire work after the area in Scotland where most of it was made, Irish firms also became involved in the work. Many trade samplers for Ayrshire work must have been made, but presumably few were considered worth preserving. However, two Scottish pieces have been found, one containing about thirty numbered designs worked mostly in chain stitch with a tambour hook. On it are handkerchief corners, skirt flounces, borders and all-over sprigged patterns. This would probably have been reproduced on muslin stretched on a large frame in a work room. The second piece contains some eighty needlepoint fillings, worked in differently shaped spaces, in lines of eight, each numbered in ink, and would probably have been copied by country women in their own homes. An agent would collect and pay for the work and take it back to the manufacturer to be made up into items of clothing.

This industy was destroyed partly by changes in fashion, but also by the invention of machinery to do the embroidery. In 1829 Henry Houldsworth of Manchester had bought the rights to a machine invented by Josue Heilmann of Mulhouse. Houldsworth improved the machine and by 1859 had twenty in operation. Although one or two other British firms had similar machines, Houldsworth had a virtual monopoly until 1875 when more advanced machines from a Swiss manufacturer were introduced. The technology for designing sewing machines was developing simultaneously in several countries, but it was Isaac M. Singer of

Pittstown, New York, who in 1851 first patented a machine which displayed many characteristics of the modern domestic sewing machine.

From the 1830s onwards almost all other forms of needlework were eclipsed by a rage for Berlin woolwork, so called because the wool and patterns for the designs originated in that German city. The first coloured designs on check or graph paper that characterized this needlework were apparently published in 1804–5 by a Berlin printseller named Philipson.

A good example of Berlin woolwork, mid-nineteenth century.

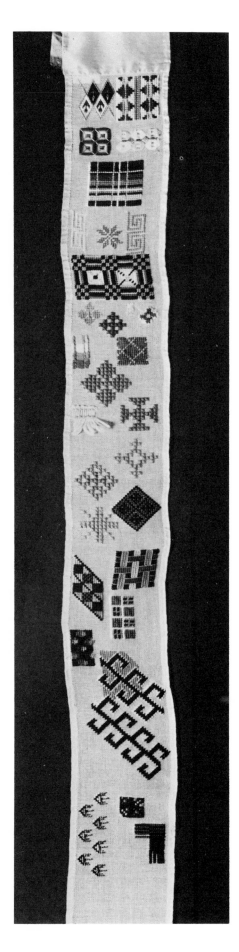

## Samplers

The patterns were not especially popular until 1831, when a London publisher purchased a large number of patterns and materials from Berlin. By 1840, 14,000 coloured designs on squared paper had been published.

The popularity of Berlin woolwork derived partly from the patterns, which were easy to follow simply by counting and enabled the worker to achieve a high degree of realism through shading, and partly because the wools sold to accompany them were much softer and took a more brilliant, faster dye than the hard-twisted worsteds previously available.

Great improvements had already been made in the science of dyeing in the first half of the nineteenth century but in 1856 an English chemist, William Henry Perkins, accidentally discovered a lavender dye made from aniline, a coal tar product. This discovery created great excitement in England and the new colour was called mauve. Tradition has it that to celebrate the discovery Queen Victoria wore a mauve dress, penny-postage stamps were dyed mauve, and London policemen were heard telling loiterers to 'get a mauve on'.

Berlin woolwork designs immediately took advantage of the new colours such as magenta, blues, violets and greens. The *Englishwoman's Domestic Magazine* generally carried a pattern for such items as a foot stool, gentlemen's slippers, a sofa pillow, lady's purse, fire screen, bellpull or pincushion to be made in this manner. In the July 1862 issue it gave the following advice along with the pattern: 'The shades should be selected of the brightest possible colours and all the gold portions of the pattern should be done in filoselle to give the work a richer appearance.'

Berlinwork was often enhanced with either silk thread or beads or both. Beadwork enjoyed something of a revival in its own right in the late nineteenth century but was often used in conjunction with Berlin-work. The influence of Berlinwork is easily noted on children's samplers, which, by the end of the century, often contained floral bouquets of large blooms, buildings, or the domestic pets which were extremely popular for working on cushions and firescreens. They would also include the conventional inscription, date and signature.

But there also exists a group of long woolwork samplers containing many different floral and geometric patterns worked on a characteristic white double canvas. It is thought that these were worked by skilled adult needlewomen, and perhaps sold in the fancy needlecraft shops for amateurs to copy. But it is equally possible that they were reference sheets for the professional embroiderer herself. These pieces displayed a wide variety of stitches, chiefly cross, tent, satin, hungarian, florentine and brick with some couching, laid and plush work. They were made on

On the Death of my Affectionate Mother.

long, narrow canvas strips usually bound at the edges with silk ribbons and sometimes with a piece of silk attached to the top to cover the sampler when rolled up.

These samplers bear some relationship both in concept and form to the seventeenth-century random pieces and so, in one sense, samplers had returned to their original function. However, the florid designs of Berlinwork were, almost from the beginning, held in very low regard by the contemporary arbiters of taste. The work was criticized for requiring copying skills only and for stultifying originality: also, a new interest in the study of old embroidery resulted in a fashion for the subtle, faded colours of those pieces as against the brilliant hues of Berlin wools.

Some of the most vociferous attacks on Berlinwork came from churchmen and church architects, who were now taking a particular interest in embroidery following the Catholic Emancipation Act of 1829. This Act resulted in the building and subsequent furnishing of many new churches. Augustus Welby Northmore Pugin, the great Gothic revival-ist architect, wrote that women's needlework appeared to be inspired by little more than Valentine letters: 'We must earnestly impress on all those who work in any way for the decoration of the altar that the only hope of reviving the perfect style is by strictly adhering to ancient auth-orities, illuminated manuscripts, stained glass and especially brasses.'

In 1871 the Church Extension Association was set up in London for the promotion of church needlework. The Association offered samplers of suitable stitches for church embroidery and, for a modest price, would also hire out patterns with the colours and stitches indicated.

The fashion for studying historic embroideries was embodied in what became known as the Art Needlework Movement. A major by-product of this was the setting up in 1872 of the Royal School of Art Needlework under the active patronage of Princess Christian, Queen Victoria's third daughter. The school had the double aim of providing employment for poor gentlewomen in the sewing repair rooms and improving the general standards of embroidery. Similarly inspired by the movement was an influential volume published in 1882 and entitled *Needlework as Art* by Lady Marian Alford, a gifted embroideress. The craze for Art Needlework, like Berlinwork before it, also spread to America, where similar schools were established with several teachers sent from England. The style promoted by such institutions ultimately eroded the popularity of Berlinwork. However, just as the Art Needlework movement was at its zenith, it too was attacked for being 'museum-inspired' and for ignoring nature as it really was.

But in spite of the changing dictates of fashion, 'Fancy Work' retained a steady popularity throughout the century. Enormous numbers of small objects were made using a combination of unusual embroidery materials and highly original techniques. Innumerable patterns were printed in the various ladies' magazines not only for embroidery but also for crochet, netting, tatting, macramé, braidwork, appliqué, knitting, painting and woodwork, none of which had any need of samplers. And many of these crafts made use of the new raw materials available to nineteenth-century needlewomen, including irridiscent beetle wings from India, fish scales, feathers, beads and many types of ribbon. Fancy work reached a peak in the 1880s but from the 1890s Art Nouveau was all the rage.

Marcus B. Huish, writing about samplers in 1900 as the outcome of an exhibition held at The Fine Art Society in London that year had some scathing comments to make about nineteenth-century examples. He wrote:

One sampler dated within the last half century finds a place in this book, but it is indeed a degraded object, and is included here to show to what the fashion had come in the Victorian era, an era notable for huge sums being expended on Art schools, and over a million children receiving Art instruction at the nation's expense. The sampler is dated 1881, and was the work of a lady of seventeen years of age. The groundwork is a common handkerchief, the young needlewoman evidently considering that its puce-coloured printed border was a better design than any she could invent. It was produced at a school, for there are broidered upon it the names of thirty-five other girls, besides seven bearing her own patronymic ... It is adorned with no less than nine alphabets, not one of which contains an artistic form of lettering. As to the ornament, the cross and anchor hustle the pawnbroker's golden balls, and formless leaves surround the single word 'love', all that the maker's invention could supply of sentimentality. This is apparently the best that the deft fingers of Art-taught girlhood could then produce. The flash in the pan that, round about the date of its creation, was leading to the production of the 'chairback' in crewels, collapsed before machine-made imitations, and well it might when even a knowledge of how to stitch an initial is unnecessary as we can obtain by return of post from Coventry, at the price of a shilling or so a hundred, a roll of our names in red, machine-worked, lettering ...

The decay of needlework amongst the children of the middle classes may perhaps be counterbalanced by other useful employments, but undoubtedly with those of a lower stratum of society the lack of it has simply resulted in their filling the blank with the perusal of a cheap literature, productive of nothing that is beneficial either to mind or body.

It was some years before a widespread revival of needlework took place, but it is probably wrong to ascribe to machines total blame for the decline. Arguably, the introduction of machine-made embroidery and other sewing techniques has stimulated the revival of modern-day needlework. From that point it became possible for the routine parts of sewing to be completed quickly by machine, leaving the decorative finishing touches to be handsewn and women with more time for their other tasks.

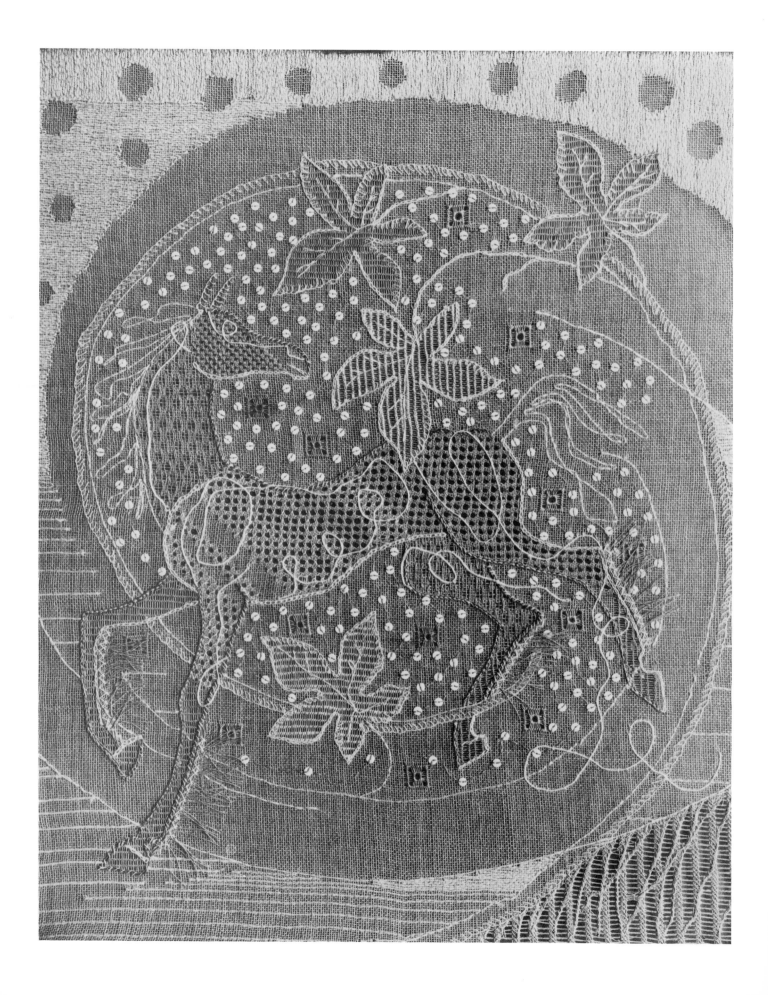

# 6
# Modern Samplers

The salient feature of the first half of much of the twentieth-century world was the effect produced by two world wars in the space of less than thirty years. Wartime quickened the pace of social change in Britain in so profound a manner that already, after the First World War, the halcyon days of the privileged orders had been swept away. Once it was finally realized that the glittering days and nights of Edwardian high society had gone forever, and that the abundance of cheap domestic servants was to be hardly more than a faint memory, there appeared to be a tendency towards more egalitarianism. This was, for many years, largely illusory, but several important factors which helped create the illusion have a bearing on the development of needlework.

In the first place, wartime blurred the distinctions between the sexes. Women had shown themselves to be responsible beings, vital to the smooth running of the economy. Almost as soon as war was declared in 1914 the London Society for Women's Suffrage changed its name and its aims to become the London Society for Women's Service, a free bureau to advise women of all ages about how they could most usefully help the war effort. Women who became tramway conductors, lift attendants, bookstall clerks, ticket collectors, motor van drivers, guards and milk deliverers enjoyed independence as never before, while those allowed to work in highly-paid jobs in munition factories were among the first of their sex to earn a wage on which a family could live. At the same time, female nurses and VADs (Voluntary Aid Detachments) focused attention on women as the heroines of the war. Partly in gratitude for all this and partly to forestall any renewed women's militancy, an Act granting partial female suffrage was passed in 1918. Women's emancipation was, however, not a luxury but a necessity. The war had

OPPOSITE A sparse but engaging English design worked in linen threads on linen, with sequins, by Rebecca Compton in 1938.

ABOVE A half-apron sewing sampler made for the City and Guilds examinations in needlework.
BELOW Pupil-teacher Janet Forsyth's 1905 sampler, worked in red silk on linen and bound at the sides in red silk ribbon.

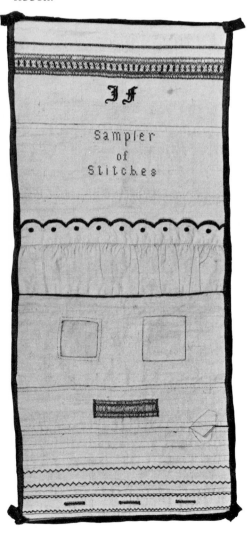

## Samplers

killed almost a generation of men, leaving many women destined either to be spinsters responsible for their own livelihoods or widows responsible for fatherless children as well as themselves.

In the immediate aftermath of the war, women's fashions emphasized the new spirit of emancipation. The 'schoolboy shape' of short, cropped hair, flat chests, thin shoulders and cylindrical skirts predominated. For a while, femininity and maternal instincts were exaggeratedly ignored. But, although both feminine charms and curves returned in the 1930s, some of the steps towards freedom could not be eroded and several of the older conventions were relaxed for good.

New synthetics were introduced, which meant that underwear for men and women was lighter and briefer and rarely hand-made. Suddenly women of all classes could buy more clothes that were cheap and yet attractive.

If women were to be responsible for their own destiny the essential concomitant was that they had to be educated, at least to the same standards as men. This was a slow process, however; by 1925–26 the University of Cambridge had just 475 women out of 5203 men and Oxford had 820 out of 4353.

An important step towards the better academic education of women was the gradual weeding of needlework from the curriculum. Of course, it still persisted and does so even today in many schools, but it is rarely accorded its old importance.

Until about 1920, most schoolgirls would still, at an early age, make an alphabet sampler, probably of cross stitch only in wool on canvas. If this contained any pictorial elements at all they would usually bear a close resemblance to those of a bygone age since the sampler was probably copied from an old one, kept in a schoolroom drawer and brought out for just such a purpose.

One innovation in sampler-making, introduced towards the end of the nineteenth century, persisted for the first two decades of the twentieth. This was the plain sewing sampler, a collection of mending and dressmaking processes such as gathering, buttonholing, taking tucks, inserting gussets and attaching tapes. These unpretentious samplers originated in the charity schools and orphanages and later became part of the curriculum in the specialist schools of domestic science and needlework. They became an essential part of the needlework examinations for the City and Guilds of London Institute and many other schools of art. Although domestic sewing machines became more common after 1860, many clothes were made by hand until the 1920s.

Many of the plain sewing samplers were in the shape of an irregular

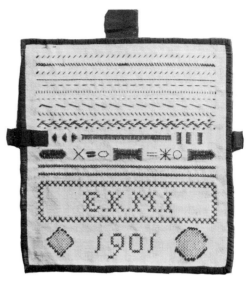

apron or half shirt and might be made on fine lawn or muslin, or else flannel or calico – the materials for most hand-made underwear until synthetics became widely available in the '30s. Most of them were signed, sometimes with initials only, but few were dated. Many were probably made by pupil–teachers, partly as proof of their technical ability and partly to be used for teaching. Janet Forsyth, a pupil–teacher at an Edinburgh school, worked a rectangular sampler of this type in red silk thread in about 1905. She included examples of cross, buttonhole, satin, eyelet hole, feather, back and overcast stitches as well as some drawn threadwork, tucks, a pocket, two patches, a gusset and various edgings. She bound the sides with red silk ribbon, ending in tiny bows at top and bottom, and inscribed the piece 'JF Sampler of Stitches'. A sampler worked by 'EKMI' in 1901 for the City and Guilds examination is in the conventional square shape, but was probably intended for teaching since the stitches are all exaggerated in size. This piece is also bound with ribbon and shows a variety of sewing stitches and processes. Another sampler of this type, by B. Hodnett *c.* 1890, and almost 3.75 metres (12½ feet) long, includes examples of knitting in addition to plain sewing, crochet and embroidery, all of which were attached in a continuous line. This piece is trimmed with machine-made lace and blue ribbon.

ABOVE A sharp, clear record of a variety of stitches, worked in 1901 for the City and Guilds examination.

BELOW Janet Ness' sampler of darning stitches, *c.* 1835. Worked in cotton thread on cotton net.

A variation on the theme of a plain sewing sampler was a piece that showed stitches and ways to use them and build them into patterns, rather than a variety of patterns and designs. Often the rows would be left half-finished to show exactly how the stitches were worked. Many well-known teachers of needlework favoured the use of this type of stitch sampler and this method of teaching is still practised today.

A sampler of darning stitches on cotton net, mounted on blue paper for clarity, was made by Janet Inglis Ness in the 1930s. Janet Ness was a teacher at the Glasgow College of Domestic Science and this sampler was probably used to explain the stitches to students.

One of the most famous needlework teachers to promote samplers as a means of teaching was Mrs Archibald Christie. In her book *Samplers and Stitches*, published in 1920, she wrote that her aim was to make workers take some characteristic stitches and see what could be done with them, rather than to make a design with a pencil and brush and then see what stitches could be adapted to working it out. 'The former method is fairly certain to result in a true embroidery design, the latter sometimes looks as if it was stitched with difficulty and would perhaps have been better if painted with a brush.'

Mrs Christie, who taught embroidery at the Royal College of Art

ABOVE 'The Wayside', from Mrs Archibald Christie's book *Samplers and Stitches*, includes chain, bullion knot, buttonhole and overcast stitches.
BELOW Blackwork by Mrs Mary Fry.

OPPOSITE Mrs Louisa Robins of Cathays, Cardiff, composed the verses for her sampler to commemorate the Coronation of George VI in 1937.

## Samplers

in London, believed that any good embroiderer should have a store of stitch knowledge from which to choose so as to vary the texture of the piece being worked. 'When considering a new piece of work it is a good plan to have a sampler of stitches to look at', she wrote. In defining her view of the ideal sampler she said:

The elements of which it is composed should be arranged with sufficient order and design to make it pleasing to look upon, to be an object worthy to be framed and hung upon a wall. From the useful point of view it can be a record of stitches and ways of using them. This is accomplished by working rows of stitches in line, which, in a panel below can be applied to suitable objects such as birds, flower sprigs or geometrical figures. The sampler should also be a record of patterns and colour schemes; fragments of these may be a sufficient reminder. It can contain a motley collection of useful elements gleaned from many sources. An alphabet should have a place upon it, for sometimes verses have to be worked or linen needs to be marked.

To emphasize her point, Mrs Christie included throughout the book stitch samplers in pictorial patterns entitled 'A Meadow', 'A Park', 'The Jungle', 'The Wayside' and 'The Harvest Field'. Also shown were a number of practical stitch samplers.

Louisa Pesel, one-time director of the Royal Hellenic Schools of Needlework and Laces in Athens, was another teacher in the early part of the century who put great store by samplers, both old and new. By 1931, Miss Pesel had completed a collection of kneelers, stall and chair cushions for the private chapel of the Bishop of Winchester at Wolvesey, all based on designs adapted from seventeenth-century samplers. After this she organized about two hundred workers, The Winchester Cathedral Broderers, to make kneelers and seat cushions for the Cathedral itself. These pieces, made in what has come to be known as Winchester Cathedral Work, were copied from some stitch samplers especially made for the project.

Many contemporary teachers of adult needlework classes find the sampler as essential an adjunct to the book as the blackboard is to the teacher of elementary arithmetic. Mrs Mary Fry of New Jersey teaches all kinds of embroidery to women aged twenty to seventy. Her method is first to demonstrate a stitch and then to make the student reproduce it on a specially devised sampler. This enables the students to learn far more stitches and ways of using them than if they had brought in their own designs to work. Only after a large assortment of stitches has been mastered on a sampler do Mrs Fry's students design their own projects.

The twentieth century has seen a widespread revival of practical samplers used by those involved in church decoration or in preparations

FOR GEORGE VI
    OUR EMPEROR KING,
THE BELLS THROUGHOUT
    THE EMPIRE RING,
IN STITCHERY WE HERE
    RECORD
THE CROWNING OF OUR
    SOVEREIGN LORD.

IN CAMP THE YOUTHS
    OF BRITAIN FIND
THE HUMAN TOUCH,
    THE KINGLY MIND.

IN HIS OWN REALM HE FOUND HIS BRIDE,
BELOVED QUEEN, HER COUNTRY'S PRIDE.
EACH DAUGHTER, IN HER SMILING FACE,
SHOWS CHILDHOOD'S MOST ENDEARING
    GRACE.

NEVER, SINCE THE WORLD BEGAN,
CAME GREATER HERITAGE TO MAN.
EMPIRE AND THE MOTHERLAND
IN COMMON CAUSE TOGETHER STAND.

PEACE FROM THE CARES OF STATE,
ONCE THROUGH THE GARDEN GATE.

GOOD HEALTH
    UNTO THEIR MAJESTIES
WITH HONOUR, HAPPINESS, AND PEACE,
UNCOUNTED LOYAL SUBJECTS SING
LONG MAY HE REIGN-
    GOD SAVE THE KING.

# ADAM

ANNE

Monday, 15th May, 1978

ARK

The inner side
of every cloud is
bright and shining.
I therefore turn
my clouds about and
always wear them
inside out
to show the lining.

Artesian Road.

Columbia Heights

LEFT Two examples of ecclesiastical samplers with elaborate goldwork from the Royal School of Needlework. The crucifix in the lower example has been left unfinished.

for special royal occasions. As in Elizabethan days when gold and silver were so popular, metallic thread is still costly and difficult to use, requiring experience. A sampler worked by Miss Louisa M. Chart while at the Royal School of Needlework in London illustrates ten different types of gold, silver and metal threads as well as coloured silk thread in various couching and laidwork stitches. Inscribed on cards to accompany the piece are the words: 'Ecclesiastical sampler Louisa M. Chart' and, beneath the motif of a rose on a stem, 'ROSE worked according to method on Elizabethan Bible, Bodleian Library – Oxford'. Another card includes some threads – 'Samples of gold threads used'. Miss Chart, who taught embroidery in the School of Design and Crafts at Edinburgh College of Art from 1914–43, made this a real working sampler as she wrote a complete set of notes on the stitches and the working of the motifs to accompany the piece.

OPPOSITE A colourful sampler worked by the author's mother-in-law, Rosalie Sebba, to commemorate the birth of her grandchild. The houses show Adam's two homes in London and New York; the clock indicates his time of birth.

*Samplers*

Other samplers of this type show the use of jewels and spangles on rich materials such as figured silk damask or velvet. A piece with silk, gold thread and spangles on purple velvet was made in 1952 to illustrate the designs and methods for the embroidery on the Coronation Robe of Queen Elizabeth II.

Individual workers with special interests in embroidery have always made and kept samplers as reference sheets of their experiments with particular techniques. For example, some extremely modern work has been done in couching down gold and silver threads with those of different colours and textures. The technique can be exploited to make quite distinct effects, whether stark geometrical shapes or loose flowing rivers of thread are required. Another technique which has never really lost its appeal in Britain since the sixteenth century, is blackwork. Almost any design can be divided into irregular areas, each one worked in a slightly different form of blackwork, to become an attractive sampler picture. The success of this type of design depends largely on the emphasis given to these areas by their shape and tone. Patterns can be made darker in tone simply by using a thicker thread and the shapes can be planned by experimenting with pieces of newspaper. Almost any motif can be used for the outline shape – maps work particularly well – and the border patterns of seventeenth-century samplers may provide a good source of inspiration for the fillings.

There is a fashion today for sampler kits, which are usually sold with the pattern already stamped on the evenweave linen or canvas, a guide supplied as to the suggested stitches as well as the required wool or thread. Sometimes transfers are sold for the worker to iron on the design herself. These kits are generally held in low regard by needlework teachers as they leave no room for the worker's creativity or imagination. But they are a good way for children, who might not otherwise be able to design a sampler, to learn the fun of sampler-making. Many of these kits are made to commemorate special national occasions such as a coronation or jubilee. Several kits were made available on the Coronation of King George VI in 1937. The spring 1937 number of *The Embroideress* included three Coronation samplers as well as one illustrating the Jubilee of King George V two years previously.

The kit samplers have also become popular with museums and stately homes, many of which have had pieces designed based on historic embroideries in their possession. Even without kits, commemorative samplers have been more popular with twentieth-century needlewomen than those of other centuries. The end of the First World War was the inspiration for at least one piece dated 28 June 1919. This included a poem

A good example of how any design can be broken up into quite distinct areas with different techniques of blackwork.

Behold he cometh leaping upon the mountains skipping upon the hills.

T from E 1934

This modern gift sampler was made by Eleanor Butler Roosevelt for her husband Brigadier General Theodore Roosevelt Jr. Like his father President Theodore Roosevelt, he was an ardent hunter. The sampler is worked in half cross stitch on canvas, and its colours are subtle.

celebrating the Allied victory and the return of peace and motifs in keeping with the theme, such as a cottage with flowers, a man gardening and a lady feeding birds and animals.

For American needleworkers one of the most stirring events of the early part of the century was the first non-stop solo airplane flight from New York to Paris made by Charles A. Lindbergh in May 1927. Several sampler maps were made at this time tracing the route taken by Lindbergh's aircraft, The Spirit of St Louis.

As leisure time has increased in the twentieth century the hobby of needlepoint, especially in the United States, is enjoying a huge following.

## Modern Samplers

For women of many countries designing and making a sampler can provide the ideal antidote to the pressures of modern life. Most of these are storytelling samplers and may rely on many of the traditional elements such as a verse, buildings, and floral motifs. But they generally record events such as births, deaths or marriages, moves to a new land or associations with the old. The special textile paints available to twentieth-century needlewomen have proved a boon, for they make it possible to plan out every detail of the sampler in advance on the canvas without resorting to a pre-designed kit or ink that may run.

Two women in Arkansas have a flourishing business selling hand-painted sampler canvases ready to be worked. They stress the traditional aspect of their samplers by attaching written histories of the designs; but as the painting is done thread by thread, the worker must adhere to someone else's ideas about colour and shading. One sampler designed by these women includes the following contemporary verse by Anne Campbell:

It was in this cheery kitchen
She worked the sampler fair
You'll see it hanging on my wall,
I love its presence there
When Grandma was a little girl
In days we'll never see,
She sat beside that roaring fire
And made it just for me.

In so far as the storytelling sampler of today relies on a needle and thread to record what otherwise the memory might forget, the old idea of a sampler has been revived. Now that women's academic education is, in most cases, struggling to be equivalent to men's, samplers are unlikely ever again to be used as an essential part of a school curriculum. But the passage of time has already made it possible to view needlework more objectively and those women who happily sit sewing probably do so through choice rather than compulsion. For them, as for the teachers and experts in needlework, making a sampler is too valuable a pursuit to be consigned to the realms of history and, in some form, the craft will probably always be with us.

# Cleaning Methods

In the *Dictionary of Needlework* by Sophia F. Caulfeild and Blance L. Saward, published in 1882, the following method of cleaning woolwork was suggested:

If the woolwork is not much soiled, stretch it in a frame and wash it over with a quart of water, into which a tablespoonful of ox-gall has been dropped. If much soiled wash with gin and soft soap, in the proportions of a quarter of a pound of soap to half a pint of gin. When carefully washed, stretch the work out to dry, and iron on the wrong side while it is still damp. If the woolwork is only faded, and not dirty, stretch it in a frame and sponge with a pint of warm water, into which a piece of soap the size of a walnut and a tablespoonful of ox-gall have been dropped. Wash out the mixture by sponging the work over with clean warm water, and leave in the frame until it is perfectly dry.

But modern products have produced modern methods, and I am much indebted to Ms. Mair Rees, Conservation Officer at the Textile Department of the Welsh Folk Museum, St Fagans, Cardiff, for her advice on cleaning and repair processes for old samplers, and for permission to quote her in full:

There are only two cleaning processes that I would recommend for samplers – suction cleaning and washing. Suction or vacuum cleaning is the least harmful for the textile and will remove all loose, air-borne dirt. First of all, the sampler is covered with a nylon monofilament screening (or any similar smooth and rigid net). This keeps the sampler firmly in place, and ensures that no loose threads can be pulled out whilst the nozzle of a vacuum cleaner sucks gently over the surface collecting all the dust and dirt. This vacuum cleaning process is also carried out before washing dirty textiles.

Washing is advisable *only after every coloured embroidery thread has been tested for colour fastness.* I usually hunt around the reverse side of the sampler looking for small coloured thread ends which can be snipped off. These are then placed on a white sheet of absorbent paper and another sheet placed on top. The two sheets are then wetted with the proposed washing solution (de-ionized water and anionic detergent) and allowed to dry naturally.

If any dyes are fugitive, they will transfer their colour on to the white absorbent paper; if this does occur then no further wet cleaning can take place. But, if all the dyes prove to be colour-fast, then the washing can continue.

Choose a shallow washing vessel that is large enough to take the sampler flat. (Photographic developing trays are ideal.) Sandwich the sampler between two layers of net – this will help support the textile while it is wet. My washing solution is always de-ionized water and 'Synperonic NDB' (ICI), but it is quite safe to wash a sampler in ordinary soft tap water, *as long as the final rinsing water is distilled or de-ionized.* During washing, the sampler must not be rubbed or squeezed – the only mechanical action is done by sponging gently so that the water and suds are pushed through the fibres.

The cleaned sampler is dried flat on a non-porous surface; whilst it is very wet it should be smoothed and straightened – then all the excess moisture can be removed with absorbent, acid-free paper or clean towels. It is allowed to dry naturally away from direct heat and light.

As for repairing samplers, I tend to follow the same method for all samplers (except for silk and satin embroidered maps). Once cleaned, the sampler is mounted on to a hardboard mount, which has been covered with a natural linen or cotton fabric that complements the sampler. The linen or cotton is stretched over hardboard and glued (with PVA adhesive) at the back only. Once dry, the sampler is sewn on to the front, then needs only to be framed and glazed. It must be remembered that the glass and the sampler should be kept apart – a narrow fillet of acid-free card inside the frame will ensure this.

There are a few things to be kept in mind when planning where to display samplers in the home. The temperature and humidity should be fairly constant – around 20°C temperature and 55% RH [relative humidity] is recommended. Light can cause a lot of damage to a delicate sampler – it should be kept out of direct sunlight and strong daylight. If artificial lights are to be used to illuminate the specimen, then tungsten lamps are preferred as they do not emit ultraviolet radiation. Flourescent lamps would have to be filtered as they do emit UV rays.

# Glossary of Stitch Designs

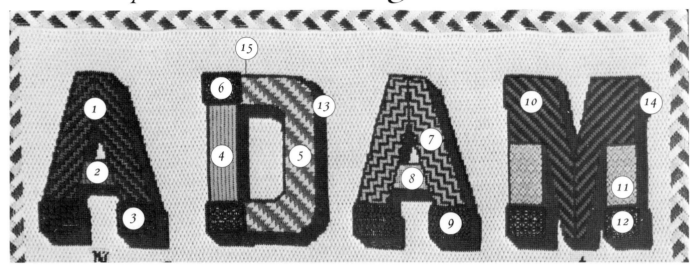

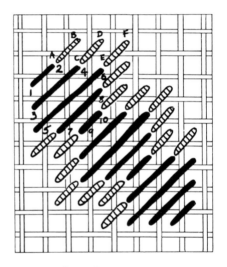

1 Moorish stitch

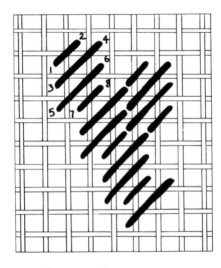

2 Cashmere stitch

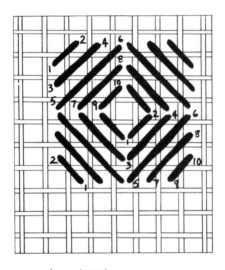

3 Cushion (UK) or
  Scotch (USA) stitch

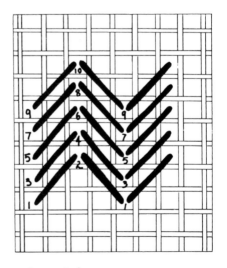

4 Stem stitch

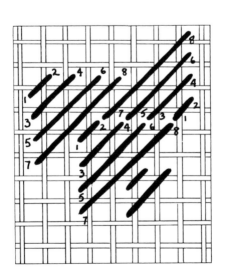

5 Milanese

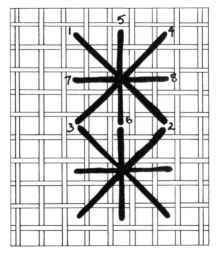

6 Smyrna cross stitch

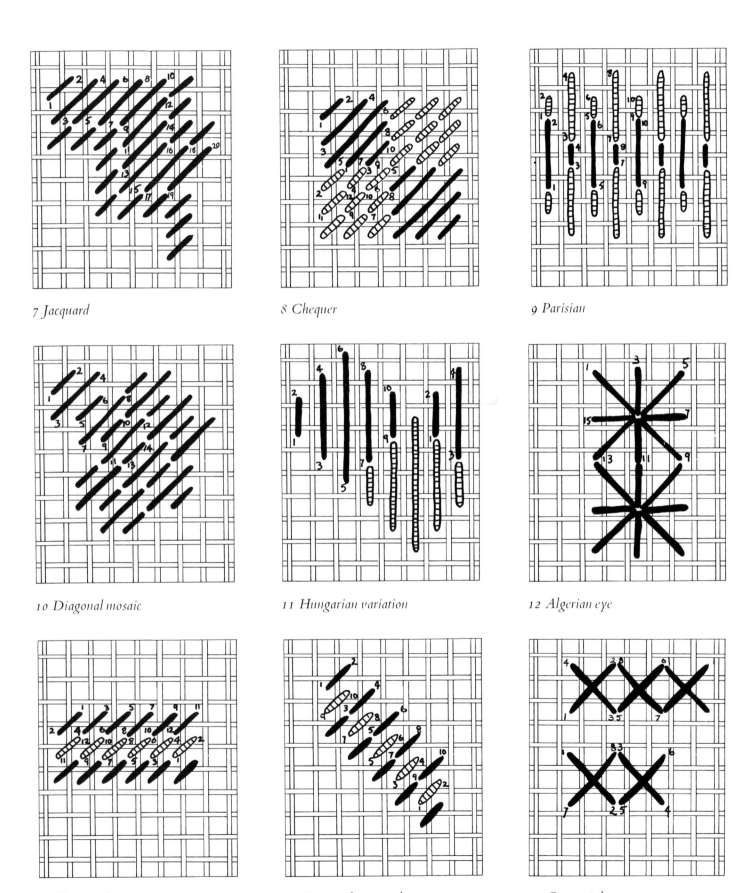

7 Jacquard

8 Chequer

9 Parisian

10 Diagonal mosaic

11 Hungarian variation

12 Algerian eye

13 Tent stitch

14 Diagonal tent stitch

15 Cross stitch

*Only four of the crewel stitches shown on this page have been used in the houses.*

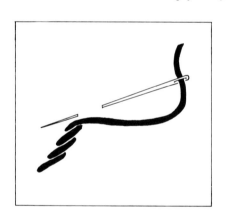

*1 Stem stitch*

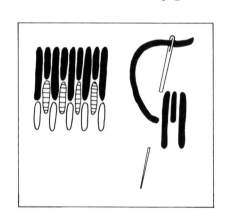

*2 Long and short stitch*

*3 Chain stitch*

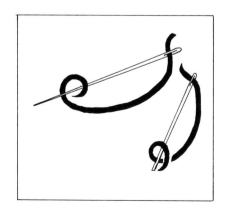

*4 French knot*

*5 Back stitch*

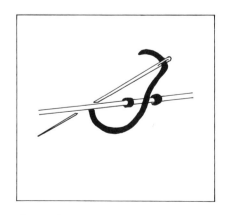

*6 Couching*

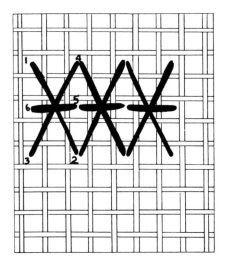

7 Tied oblong cross stitch

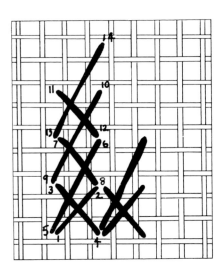

8 Long armed cross stitch

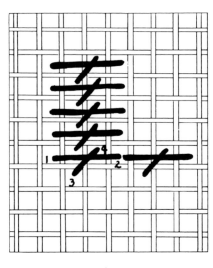

9 Rumanian stitch

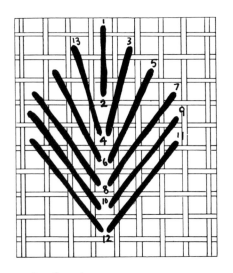

10 Leaf stitch

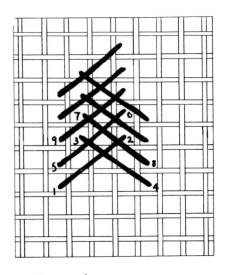

11 Fern stitch

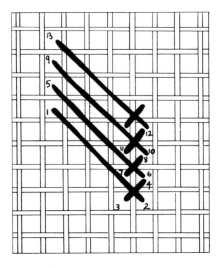

12 Fishbone

# Select Bibliography

ADROSKO, Rita J. *Natural dyes in the U.S.* U.S. National Museum Bulletin no 281, 1968.

ASHTON, Sir Arthur. *Samplers.* Medici Society: London & Boston 1926.

BOLTON, Ethel Stanwood and Coe, Eva Johnston. *American samplers.* National Society of the Colonial Dames of America: Massachusetts Branch 1921.

BROWN, Harbeson Georgiana. *American needlework: the history of decorative stitchery from the late sixteenth to twentieth century.* Coward McCann: New York 1938.

BURROWS, Swan Susan. *A Winterthur guide to American needlework.* Crown Publishers Inc: New York 1976.

BURROWS, Swan Susan. *Plain and fancy. American women and their needlework 1700–1850.* Holt, Rinehart and Winston: New York 1977.

CAULFEILD, Sophia Frances Anne and Saward, Blance C. *The dictionary of needlework.* L. Upcott Gill: London 1882.

CHRISTIE, A Grace I. *Samplers and stitches.* B. T. Batsford: London 1921.

CLABBURN, Pamela. *Samplers.* Shire Publications: Bucks 1977.

COLBY, Averil. *Samplers.* B. T. Batsford: London 1964.

DREESMAN, Cecile. *Samplers for today.* Van Nostrand Rheinhold: New York 1972.

ENTHOVEN, Jacqueline. *The stitches of creative embroidery.* Rheinhold: New York 1964.

FINCH, Karen and Putnam, Greta. *Caring for textiles.* Barrie and Jenkins: London 1977.

GARRETT, Elizabeth D. 'American samplers and needlework pictures in the DAR museum'. Part I: 1739–96. *Antiques* no 105, 1974. Part II: 1804–40. *Antiques* no 107, 1975.

GOTTESMAN, Rita Susswein. *The arts and crafts in New York, 1726–1776.* Historical Society: New York 1938.

GROW, Judith K. and MCGRAIL, Elizabeth. *Creating historic samplers.* Pyne Press: Princeton, 1974.

HAIG, Elizabeth. *The floral symbolism of the great masters.* Kegan Paul & Co: London 1913.

HOLE, Helen G. *Westtown through the years.* Westtown Alumni Association 1942.

HORNER, Marianna Merritt. *The Story of samplers.* Philadelphia Museum of Art: Philadelphia 1963.

HUISH, Marcus Bourne. *Samplers and tapestry embroideries.* Longmans & Co: London 1900.

JEWISH MUSEUM, The. *The fabric of Jewish life. Textiles from the Jewish Museum Collection*: New York 1977.

JONES, Mary Eirwen. *British samplers.* Pen-in-Hand: Oxford 1948.

JOURDAIN, Margaret. *The history of English secular embroidery.* Kegan Paul & Co: London 1910.

KASSEL, Hilda. *Stitches in time: the art and history of embroidery.* Duell, Sloan and Pearce: New York 1966.

KENDRICK, Albert. *English needlework.* A. & C. Black: London 1933.

KING, Donald. 'The earliest dated sampler'. *Connoisseur*, vol CXLIX no 234: London 1936.

KING, Donald. *Samplers.* Victoria and Albert Museum: London 1960.

KING, Donald. 'Boxers'. *Embroidery*, vol XII, no 4: 1961.

KRUEGER, Glee. *A gallery of American samplers.* E. P. Dutton in association with the Museum of American Folk Art: New York 1978.

KRUEGER, Glee. *New England samplers to 1840.* Old Sturbridge Village: Sturbridge, Massachusetts 1978.

LEENE, Jentina E. *Textile conservation.* Butterworths: London 1972.

LEVEY, Santina. *Discovering embroidery of the nineteenth century.* Shire Publications: Bucks 1971.

LIPMAN, Jean and Winchester, Alice. *The flowering of American folk art 1776–1876.* Viking Press in cooperation with the Whitney Museum of American Art: New York 1974.

LOTHROP, Samuel Kirkland. *Essays in pre-Columbian art and archaeology.*

Harvard University Press: Cambridge, Massachusetts 1961.

MIEULENBELT-NIEUWBURG, Alberta. *Embroidery motifs from Dutch samplers.* B. T. Batsford: London 1974.

MONTGOMERY, Charles F. and KANE, Patricia E. General editors of *American art 1750–1800: towards Independence.* New York Graphic Society: Boston 1976.

MORRIS, Barbara. *Victorian embroidery.* Herbert Jenkins: London 1962.

ODDY, Revel. *Samplers in the Guildford Museum.* Guildford Museum: Guildford, Surrey 1951.

PALLISER, Fanny Bury. *History of lace.* Sampson Low & Co: London 1875.

PAYNE, F. G. *Samplers and embroideries in the National Museum of Wales.* National Museum of Wales: Cardiff 1939.

RING, Betty. 'Collecting American samplers today'. *Antiques* no 101, 1972.

RING, Betty. 'The Balch school in Providence, Rhode Island'. *Antiques* no 107, 1975.

SCHIFFER, Margaret Berwind. *Historical needlework of Pennsylvania.* Charles Scribner & Sons: New York 1968.

SWAIN, Margaret H. *The Flowerers. The origins and history of Ayrshire needlework.* W. R. Chambers London and Edinburgh 1955.

SWAIN, Margaret H. *Historical needlework: a study of influences in Scotland and northern England.* Barrie & Jenkins: London 1970.

TARRANT, Naomi. *The Royal Scottish Museum samplers.* Royal Scottish Museum: Edinburgh 1978.

VINCIOLO, Frederico. *An unabridged facsimile of the 'Singuliers et nouveaux pourtraicts' of 1587.* Dover publications: New York 1971.

WADE, N. Victoria. *The basic stitches of embroidery.* Victoria and Albert Museum: London 1960.

WARDLE, Patricia. *Guide to English embroidery.* Victoria and Albert Museum: London 1970.

# Acknowledgements

I am greatly indebted to a number of people for helping me in my research. The principal sampler collections are housed in museums in Britain and the United States of America, and the textile departments have provided me with much valuable assistance. In Britain, I should like to thank Mr Donald King, Keeper of Textiles and his staff at the Victoria and Albert Museum, Mr Robin Crighton, Keeper of Applied Arts and his staff at the Fitzwilliam Museum, Cambridge, Dr Ilid Anthony, Assistant Keeper-in-charge, Department of Domestic and Corporate Life, and her staff at the Welsh Folk Museum, Cardiff, Miss Fiona Strodder, Assistant Keeper of Social History, Strangers Hall Museum, Norwich. I am particularly grateful to Miss Mair Rees, Conservation Officer, Welsh Folk Museum for her helpful comments on the renovation of old samplers which I have quoted in full in the appendix on cleaning methods. In the United States, I should like to thank Ms Anne Farnam, Curator of the Essex Institute, Massachusetts, Ms Gillian Moss, Assistant in the Textile Department, Cooper-Hewitt Museum, New York, Ms Katharine Kvaraceus, Curator of the Textile Department, Boston Museum of Fine Arts, Ms Cissy Grossman, Assistant Curator, Jewish Museum, New York, and the Virginia State Library.

I am also most grateful to Pastor John Hines of Essex, England, Miss Phyllis Sadler, Westtown School, Pennsylvania and Professor Junius Bird, American Museum of Natural History, New York, who all shared with me their knowledge of particular aspects of samplers. I should like to extend special thanks to my Editor Kate Dunning, for her practical help and interest throughout, to Julia Brown, Picture Editor, for her unremitting work on the illustrations and Jane Stevens, compiler of the stitch glossary. My parents were of invaluable assistance in a number of ways, when I was in both London and New York. Finally, I should like to thank my husband, without whose encouragement and constructive criticism this book would never have been written.

**100** The Henry Francis du Pont Winterthur Museum, Delaware.

**101** The Henry Francis du Pont Winterthur Museum, Delaware.

**103** Museum of the City of New York.

**104** Cooper-Hewitt Museum, The Smithsonian Institution's National Museum of Design, New York.

**106** The Daughters of the American Revolution, Washington D.C.; *Antiques Magazine.*

**107** Theodore H. Kapnek Collection reprinted from *A Gallery of American Samplers*, Glee F. Krueger (Duttons).

**108** Royal Scottish Museum, Edinburgh.

**109** above Theodore H. Kapnek Collection reprinted from *A Gallery of American Samplers*, Glee F. Krueger (Duttons).

**109** below Metropolitan Museum of Art, New York. Bequest of Mable Herbert Harper, 1957. From the Collection of Mrs Lathrop Colgate Harper.

**110** The Daughters of the American Revolution, Washington D.C.; *Antiques Magazine.*

**111** The Jewish Museum, New York. Gift of Dr Harry G. Friedman, 1945.

**112** Royal Scottish Museum, Edinburgh.

**115** *Radio Times Hulton Picture Library, London.*

**117** above Fitzwilliam Museum, Cambridge.

**117** below *Christies South Kensington, London.*

**119** Royal Scottish Museum, Edinburgh.

**120** Royal Scottish Museum, Edinburgh.

**121** above left Welsh Folk Museum, St Fagans.

**121** above right Royal Scottish Museum, Edinburgh.

**121** below Brooklyn Museum, New York; *Martin Gostelow.*

**122** Cooper-Hewitt Museum, The Smithsonian Institution's National Museum of Design, New York. Bequest of Mrs Henry E. Coe.

**123** Royal Scottish Museum, Edinburgh.

**124** Strangers Hall Museum, Norfolk.

**125** Welsh Folk Museum, St Fagans.

**126** Victoria and Albert Museum, London.

**128** Welsh Folk Museum, St Fagans.

**129** Brontë Parsonage Museum, Yorkshire.

**130** Black Museum, Scotland Yard, London.

**131** *Christies South Kensington, London.*

**132** Royal Scottish Museum, Edinburgh.

**133** Helen L. Allen Collection, University of Wisconsin, Madison.

**134** Strangers Hall Museum, Norfolk.

**135** Victoria and Albert Museum, London.

**138** Victoria and Albert Museum, London.

**140** above Strangers Hall Museum, Norfolk.

**140** below Royal Scottish Museum, Edinburgh.

**141** above Strangers Hall Museum, Norfolk.

**141** below Royal Scottish Museum, Edinburgh.

**142** above Victoria and Albert Museum, London.

**142** below Mrs Mary Fry, New Jersey.

**143** Welsh Folk Museum, St Fagans.

**144** Author's Collection, New York.

**145** above The Royal School of Needlework, London; *Angelo Hornak.*

**145** below The Royal School of Needlework, London; *Angelo Hornak.*

**147** The Royal School of Needlework, London; *Angelo Hornak.*

**148** Roosevelt Collection, New York; *Alexandra Roosevelt.*


The publisher has taken all possible care to trace and acknowledge the ownership of all the illustrations. If by chance we have made an incorrect attribution we apologize most sincerely and will be happy to correct the entry in any future reprint, provided that we receive notification.

# Index

Note: numbers in *italics* refer to illustrations

acorn and oak leaves motifs, 25, 39, 42, 44, 103
Ackworth School samplers, 121–3
acrostic samplers, 75, *75*
Adam and Eve motif, 44, 66–8, 103, 119, *119*, *120*
Aled, Tudur, 22
Alford, Lady Marian, 136
Alger, Sally, 90
Algerian eye stitch, 38, 72, 75, *126*
almanacs, 75, *75*
alphabets and numerals, 44–5, *46*, 47, *47*, 48, 50, 58, 59–60, 61, *63*, 83, 84, 101, 102, 111, *112*, 116, 119, *120*, 121, 123, 140
American eagle motif, 83, *83*, *104*, 104–5
American samplers, 9, 50–3, 81–111, 123, 136, *148*, 148–9
animal motifs, 18, 20, 30, 35, 37, *119*, *120*
Anne, Queen, 68
architectural motifs (buildings), 64, 90–1, 92, *120*, *121*, 128, *128*
Arnolds Farm, Essex, sampler map of, *73*
Art Needlework Movement, 136
Ashton, Dorothy, *89*, 89–90
Assisi work, 40
Ayrshire work, 132

Balch Academy samplers, 90–3
Balfour, Jesie, *119*
band samplers, 25, 37, 38–40, 42, 44–5, *46*, *47*, 48–9, *50*, 53, 58, 59, 60, 61
Baner, Barbara A., 93, *95*
Barley, William, 22
Barnholt, Margaret, 109
Battle of Worcester (1651), 39
beadwork, 37, 49, 134, *134*
Belcher, Mary, 105
Benneson, Eliza J., 102
Berlin woolwork, 111, *121*, 133–5
Berta, Bek, *111*
Bess of Hardwick, 20
Biblical themes, 30–1, 42, 44, 66–8, 71, 103, 111, 116, 124, 128–9
Biddle, Owen, 123
bird motifs, 11, 18, 35, 37, 63, 64, 102, *119*, *120*, 122
blackwork, 8, *19*, 19–20, 49, *142*, 146, *147*
Blake, Ann, 79
Bock, Elizabeth, 69
Body, Mary Ann, 66
Bolen, Maria, 105
border designs, 20, 38, 42, 61–2, 66
  American, 90, 93, *94*, *94*, *104*
Bostocke, Jane, 25, *26*, 27
Bosworth, Mary, 84
Bott, Sally, *89*, 90
bowknots, 102–3
'Boxers', *39*, 40, 64
boys' samplers, 60–1, *61*
Bradshaw, Susannah, 131, *131*
Brassey, Elizabeth, *74*
Bright, Lucretia, 106, *106*
Brightland, John, 59
Bristol orphanages samplers, 116
Brontë, Charlotte, Emily and Anne, 129, *129*
Brooks, Thomas, 48
Brown, Anne, 72
Brumfit, Jane, 71
Brunnell, Andrew and Elizabeth, 61
Bulgarian sampler, *10*
bullion knots, 38, *85*, *142*
Bullock, Elizabeth, 75, *75*
Burr, Cynthia, *92*
Butz, Mary, *94*

Caldwell, Sarah S., 104
Campbell, Anne, 149

Carlile, Hannah, 91
Cary, Lady Dorothy, *33*
Catchpole, Eliza Davey, 124
Catherine of Aragon, Queen, 19–20
Catholic Emancipation Act (1829), 135–6
Caulfeild, Sophia F., 118, 150
Caxton, William, 16
chain stitch, 57, 76, *142*
Chapman, Ann, 68
Charles I, King, 30, *31*
Charles II, 39
Charlotte, Princess, death of, 124
Chart, Louisa M., 145
Chartist Movement, 113, 114
chenille thread, 59, 72
chevening, 132
Christian, Princess, 136
Christie, Mrs Archibald, 141–2, *142*
Christie, Jannet, *63*
Church samplers *see* Ecclesiastical embroidery
City and Guilds examination, 140, *140*, 141, *141*
clocks (for socks and stockings), 131–2
Clowser, Anne, *52*, 61
Cole, Mary, 79
commemorative samplers, 49, 76, 130–1, *143*, 146
Compton, Rebecca, *138*
Cornwallis, Mary, *19*
Coronation samplers, *143*, 146
Cousens, E., 76
Cozzens, Eliza, 91
crewelwork, 50, 57, 61, 82, *97*
Cridland, Elizabeth, 64
Cromwell, Oliver, 39, 53
cross stitch, 9, *18*, 25, 59, 72, 75, 93, 99, 117, 121, 122, *126*
crown (coronet) motif, 38, 63, *63*, 63–4, 99, 103, 104, *112*, 121, 124
crucifix motif, 8, 25, 116, 127, *145*
Cuper, Lindsay Duncan, 60
cut and drawn threadwork, 25, 35, *36*, 37, 38, 40, 42, 44, *47*, 48, *48*, 50, 79, 109

Danish sampler, *9*
darning samplers, 75, 76–7, *77*, 101, *141*, 141
Davis, Betsy, *93*
Day, Ann, 68
Dick, Elizabeth, 76
*Dictionary of Needlework*, 118–19
Divitt, Ann, 71
Doddridge, Philip, 69, 70
Doieg, Euphemia, *123*
domestic servants, Victorian, 116
double running stitch, 7, 25, 38, 44, 60, 85
Dresden work, 109, *110*
Dudden, Mary, 71
'A Dutch Lady' (Mierevelt), *42*
dyes, 88, 134

ecclesiastical embroidery, 8, 13–14, 31, 136, 142, 145, *145*
Edlin, Martha, 48, *48*–9
Education Act (1870), 116
Edwards, Ann, *41*
Egyptian samplers, 6–7
eighteenth-century samplers, *54*, 55–79
Elizabeth I, Queen, 20, 25, 29
Elizabeth II, Queen, Coronation Robe of, 146
Ellis, Sophia, *86*
*The Embroidery and Alphabet Sampler Book*, 119–20
embroidery pictures, 30–1
England, Ann E., *98*, 102
English Civil War, 30
English, Philip, 53
Eyls, Elizabeth, 47
Eyre, Mary, 106

family record samplers, 106, *106*, 109
'Fancy Work', 136
Fenn, Ann, 46–7
Fennah, M., 124
First Congregational Church, Providence, 91, *91*
First World War, 139–40, 146, 148
Fishe, Thomas, 22
Fleetwood, Miles and Abigail, 53

florentine work, 38, *51*, 61
flower and fruit motifs, 11, 18, 37, 38, 39–40, 42, 44, 61–2, 64, 91, 93, 109, *112*, *119*, 122, *123*, 124
Forsyth, Janet, *140*, 141
Fry, Mrs Mary, 142, *142*

Gale, Walter, 57
Galligher, Mrs Leah, 94
Gardner, Mary, 69
genealogical samplers, 106, *106*, 109
George I, King, 76
George VI, King, Coronation of, *143*, 146
German samplers, 7, 8, 17–18, 23, *24*, 25
Gesner, Conrad, *Historiae Animalium* by, 20, *21*
Gibson, Helen, *120*
gift samplers, 130, *148*
Gilbert, Elizabeth, 69
Gillray's cartoon (1809), *56*
Glazebrook, Martha, 120
globe samplers, 101, *101*
Goldin, Ann, 102
Goldsmith, Oliver, 60
Gower, Anne, 50, *50*
Gower, George, 19
Grace, Sarah, 121
Grant, Lucy, 129
Grant, Martha, 124, *124*, 127
grape and vine-leaf motif, 25, 111
Gray, Margaret, 121
Gray, Mary, 84
Greame, Dorothy, *54*
Gregory, Mary, 122
Grimes, Sarah, 68–9

Hall, Mary, 47
Hall, Nancy, 90
hand towels (show towels), 100, *100*
Hart, L., 11
Haskins, Anne, 61, *62*
Hawkins, Elizabeth, 72
Heilmann, Josue, 132
hem stitch, 44, 117–18
Henderson, Robert, 60
Hessin, Christina, *100*
Hodnett, B., 141
Holbein, Hans, 20
Holbein stitch, 20
Holland, Susanna M., 102
hollie point samplers, 76, 77, *78*, 79, 109, *110*
Hollingsworth, Mary, 53
Houldsworth, Henry, 132
Hudson, John, of Newcastle, 20
Huish, Marcus B., 136–7
human hair thread, 59, 106, 129, *130*
Humphreys, Jane, 109, 117
Hunt, Eliza Ann, 106
Huss, John, 100
Hutchinson, Thomas, 82
Hyde, Laura, *83*

initials, 42, 46, 63, 64, 109, *119*, n122–3
inscriptions, 9, 45, 46, 47, 49, 53, 68–71, 79, 120, 124, *125*, 128–9
  American, 53, 90, 92, *92*, 93, 94, 99, 101, 104, 105–6, 109
Inveraray Castle, *108*
Italian samplers, 7, 8, 23, 25, *36*

James I, King, 29–30, 31, 38, 42, 61
James, Ruth, 101
Jewish American samplers, 111, *111*
Jones, Rebecca, 123

Kelley, Ann E., 94
Kemp, Hannah, 127, *128*
Kendrick, A. F., 31
Kirk, Anne, 70, *70*
knotting, 57–8
Knowles, Elizabeth, 75, *75*

lacework, 11, 25, *36*, 37, 38, 40, 42, 44, 48, 109, 117
Landis, Susana, *99*
landscapes, *62*, 64, 90, 91, *104*, 105, *121*, *126*
Larkin, William, *15*

Laud, Archbishop, 31
Le Moyne, Jacques, 17
Lee, Alice, 25, 27
Lewis, Mary, 66
Lincoln, Eunice, 90
Lindbergh, Charles A., 148
linsey-woolsey material, 88
London Society for Women's Service, 139
long woolwork samplers, 134–5
Lord's Prayer samplers, 52, 61, 64, 71
Lovett, William, 114
Lucus, Margreet, 47

machine embroidery, 132–3, 137
machine-made net backgrounds, 131
Mackett, Elizabeth, 47, 47–8
Malsey, Amy, 79
map samplers, 59, 71–5, 72, 73, 74, 101, 101–2, 120, 148
marking, 117, 118
Martin, Nabby, 90
Mary Queen of Scots, 20
May, Margaret, 44
Mayne, Jasper, 45
medallions, 122, 123, 124, 127
Meguier, Mrs Leah, 93, 95
Merritt, Jane, 123
metallic thread, 20, 25, 59, 92–3, 145, 145, 146
Millenarial movements, 127
Miller, Jean, 121, 121
Miller, Mary, 79
Miller, William, 127
Minshull, Mary, 49
Miskey, Elizabeth, 99
Moravian female seminary, USA, 100
More, Hannah, 114–15
Morgan, Margaret, 123–4, 125
Moss, Margaret, 104, 105
mourning or memorial samplers, 59, 106, 109, 124, 124, 127, 135
multiplication charts, 121, 121
Mytens, Daniel, 33

Napoleonic Wars, samplers commemorating end of, 130–1
Nazca sampler (ancient Peru), 6
Nebabri, Susan, 25
Needlepoint, 25, 36, 44
   lacework, 42, 77, 132
Needlework as Art, 136
The Needle's Excellency (Taylor), 18, 31–2, 32, 35, 49
Ness, Janet Inglis, 141, 141
Newport, Rhode Island, samplers, 102
Newton, Eliza Sophia, 120
Nine Partners Boarding School, New York, 100, 123

Old State House, Providence, 90, 92
openwork samplers, 40, 42, 44, 46
oriental patterns and designs, 57, 61
orphanage samplers, 116–17, 117, 140
Ostau, Giovanni, 17, 44
Oxburgh Hall, Norfolk, 21

parents, embroidered portraits of, 64–6, 66
Parker, Annie, 129
Parker, Clarinda, 2
Parker, Ellen, 129–30
pattern books, patterns, 8, 16, 16–18, 18, 22, 31, 44, 57, 59, 84, 119–20, 131, 136
peacock motif, 35, 63, 99, 103
Peele, Nabby Mason, 88

Penrhyn Castle, N. Wales, 121
Pennsylvania school samplers, 93–4, 94, 95, 99–101, 102, 104, 104–5, 107, 109, 123
Perkins, William Henry, 134
Pesel, Louisa, 142
Pether, Mary, 126
Philadelphia Friends, 123
Philips, Miss E., 65
Pickling, Catherine, 64
pincushions, 49, 122–3
plain sewing samplers, 140, 140–1
Pleanderleath, Betty, 67
Polk, Patty, 105
Poor Law Amendment Act (1834), 113
pouncing, 18
pounds, shillings and pence charts, 121
Pugin, Augustus Welby Northmore, 136
pupil-teachers, 115, 120, 140, 141
Puritanism, 29–30, 39, 53, 81
Putnam, Ruthey, 88–9

Quaker school samplers, 100–1, 121–3
Quentel, Peter, 16, 17, 18
Quertier, M., 122
quilting, 57, 58

Rae, Francis, 122, 122
random samplers, 23, 28, 34, 37, 37–8, 134, 135
Raymond, Elizabeth, 70
Razor, Suzannah, 110
Rebus samplers, 75, 75
religious and moral verses and inscriptions, 68–71, 120, 128–9, 129, 131
religious motifs/symbolism, 8, 11, 25, 30, 42, 44, 63, 66–8, 111, 127–9
   see also ecclesiastical embroidery
Richards, Mary Ann, 65
Richardson, Eliza, 135
Richardson, Mary, 89, 96
Riche, Barnabe, 23
Roberts, Miss D. A., 129
Robins, Mrs Louisa, 143
Robinson, Mary Ann, 1
Rooke, Elizabeth, 130–1
Roosevelt, Eleanor Butler, 148
roses, 37, 39–40, 44, 93, 106
Royal School of Art Needlework, 136, 145

'S' motif, 7, 25, 40, 44
Salter, Martha, 46, 47
sampler kits, 146
sampler letters, 59–60
   see also alphabets
sampler stitch see cross stitch
Samplers and Stitches, 141–2, 142
Sands, Eliza Amelia, 120
Sarah Stivour School, 88–9, 90, 96
satin stitch, 39, 44, 50, 59, 61, 85, 93, 126, 132
Saward, Blance, L., 118, 150
Sebba, Rosalie, 144
Second Advent Movement, 127
Seixas, Rachel, 111
seventeenth-century samplers, 29–53
Seymour, Samuel, 109
Shakespeare, William, 22–3
shepherdesses and shepherds, 68, 68, 89
Sherwin, E., 121
Schönsperger, Johannes, 17
Shorleyker, Richard, 35, 39, 50
Sibmacher, Johann, 17–18, 18, 31, 103
signatures, 25, 45, 46, 47
silk thread, 59
   black, 19–20, 59, 60
   crinkled or ravelled, 89–90

Singer, Isaac M., 132–3
Skelton, John, 22
slave sampler, 131, 131
Smith, Susan, 91
Solomon's Temple, 120, 128, 128
Spanish samplers, 7, 8, 9, 85
Speed, Eleanor, 11
Spencer, Elizabeth, 76
spot motifs, 25, 37, 38, 39, 63
Spurr, Polly, 91, 91
Stackhouse, Ellen, 75
Standish, Loara, 50, 53
Standish, Myles, 50
Stauffer, Mary Ann, 94
Steele, Ann, 129
stem stitch, 76, 93, 132
Stickney, Lucy, 81
stitch samplers, 141, 141–2
Stivour stitch, 88–9, 89
strawberry motif, 62, 66, 119
stumpwork, 31, 39, 48, 49–50

tambour work, 57, 57, 82
tammy, 59, 88
Taylor, Hannah, 97, 102
Taylor, John, 32, 35
Tchotanova, Mme, 10
tent stitch, 31, 38, 87, 119
textile paints, 149
Thomson, Margaret, of Freeston, 22
tiffany, 59, 88
Tipper, M. A., 117
trade samplers, 131, 132
Trusted, Eliza, 122
Tudor embroidery, 14–27
Turner, Polly, 92

University Hall, Providence, 90–1, 92

Varick, Mary, 103, 104
Vavassore, Giovanni Andra, 17
vellum (tacked to back of sampler), 44, 44
verses, 9, 46–7, 143, 149
   American, 50, 53, 92, 101, 102, 105–6, 109
   18th century, 59, 68–71, 79
   19th century, 116, 120, 124, 125, 128–9
Victorian samplers, 112, 113–37
Vinciolo, Federico, 17
virtue, maxims about, 92, 92, 121
'Visit to the Boarding School' (Moorland), 56

Walpole, Sir Robert, 55
Washington, George, 103, 104, 106, 109, 124
Watson, Mary Ann, 127
Watts, Dr Isaac, 63, 67, 69, 70, 71, 105, 120
weeping willow motif, 93, 95, 106, 108, 124
Welchan, Mrs, 94
Wesley, John, 69–70
Westtown School, Pennsylvania, 100–1, 123
whitework, 9, 40, 44, 47, 47, 48, 50, 79
Wilds, Amy, 69
Wilkinson, Susanna, 61
William of Orange, King, 49
Wilson, Mary V., 109
Winchester Cathedral Work, 142
Wing, Ann, 105
Winslow, Anna Green, 87
Winsor, Nancy and Olney, 92
Wolfe, John, 17
women's emancipation, 139–40
Wright, Martha, 49
Wright, Ruth, 101